Sales and Market Forecasting for Entrepreneurs

Sales and Market Forecasting for Entrepreneurs

Tim Berry

First published in 2010 by
Business Expert Press, LLC
222 East 46th Street, New York, NY 10017
www.businessexpertpress.com

ISBN-13: 978-1-60649-041-9 (paperback)
ISBN-10: 1-60649-041-9 (paperback)

ISBN-13: 978-1-60649-042-6 (e-book)
ISBN-10: 1-60649-042-7 (e-book)

DOI 10.4128/9781606490426

A publication in the Business Expert Press Small Business Management and
Entrepreneurship collection

Collection ISSN: 1946-5653 (print)
Collection ISSN: 1946-5661 (electronic)

Cover design by Artistic Group—Monroe, NY
Interior design by Scribe, Inc.

First edition: January 2010

10 9 8 7 6 5 4 3 2 1

Printed in Taiwan R.O.C.

Abstract

This book is about pragmatic, management-oriented sales forecasting for entrepreneurs, small business owners, and middle managers faced with the kind of practical management problems that forecasting can help prevent. Its main focus is the real-world sales forecast done almost every day, not using technical analysis or sophisticated forecasting techniques, but rather common sense, experience, and industry knowledge. This is forecasting that respects the educated guess.

The book is written for entrepreneurs and managers to help with practical and commonplace management issues. The sales forecast is a vital tool for management, even though it's likely to be wrong. It becomes the foundation of the expense budgets and, through that, cash management.

It begins by setting forecasting into management context. It isn't about guessing the future correctly; instead, it's about setting reasonable assumptions, getting them organized into a forecast, and then tracking and following up so that the difference between original forecast and actual results can be tracked and managed. A good forecast continues, every month, with regular review and course corrections. And that leads to better management. The process is something like steering, which is a matter of making regular corrections.

The bulk of the book is instruction by example. It presents actual cases, with step-by-step details, of sample sales forecasts. These include new products and new businesses and existing businesses. They also include top-down (called trees from the forest) forecasts from the larger market trends, and bottom-up (forest from the trees) forecasts looking at details by customer, channel, or product. These case examples are annotated with tips and traps and explanation of the underlying thinking and, where relevant, market research—and lots of spreadsheet specifics to empower the manager.

As it progresses, it does cover some of the more common sophisticated forecasting techniques, including an innovative strategic interactive model, several examples of data smoothing and weighting, and a simple regression analysis.

In the final chapter, it gathers spreadsheet forecasting tips from throughout the book to put them together where they can be most useful to real managers.

Keywords

Sales forecasting, sales forecast, forecast, business forecast, business plan, business planning, entrepreneurship, small business, small business management, plan vs. actual, variance, market segmentation, diffusion model, bottom-up forecast, top-down forecast, market forecast, market forecasting, moving average, weighted moving average, new product forecast, new business forecast, simple linear regression, unit sales, direct cost of sales, gross margin, variable cost.

Contents

CHAPTER 1

Why Bother?

This Is Business

I can't really get going with sales forecasting without writing first, to anybody running a business, about the *why* of sales forecasting. Too many people think forecasting stands alone, as if it were some ivory tower skill set based on math and research and dedicated expertise. It isn't.

Sales forecasting is really a basic tool for running a business. It's about steering a business. It's a matter of simple steps:

- First, you forecast sales.
- Then you set expense budgets, interactively, with the sales forecast. Should you increase sales and marketing expenses? Then increase projected sales—or why else would you do that? If you decrease the sales and marketing expenses, then you probably have to decrease the sales forecast too.
- As soon as you have a forecast, you begin tracking actual results. You don't expect to guess the future correctly; we're people, we don't know the future. What you do expect, instead, is to be able to see the difference between your forecasted sales and your actual sales results. What is different leads to questions and analysis on why it's different.
- Tracking results leads to managing your business better. Use the plan vs. actual analysis to adjust budgets, sales and marketing programs, inventories, and whatever else.

The sales forecast is a window to business health. As you see in the figure on the following page, many other elements of the business—in the illustration, you see costs and expenses, profits, assets and liabilities, and, most

Modification of a photo by Michael Flippo via istockphoto.com

important of all, cash flow—depend on the flow of sales. This is a matter of running the business right.

- Sales less than expected is a danger sign. Is there something going on in the environment, out in the marketplace? New competition? Changing styles and fashions? Or perhaps your own plans for sales and marketing programs haven't been implemented? Or they have, but they aren't working?
- Do you need to adjust spending budgets to deal with the sales problems? That might seem obvious, but there's the deeper problem in the underlying question: Do we spend less because sales are less than the forecast? Or do we spend smarter?

- Sales better than forecast is a much better sign, but also brings up management decisions. Does this mean there is a change in the market, competition, or styles? Will sales continue to beat the forecast? Should product lines be adjusted? Should the forecast itself be adjusted? Are sales and marketing programs working better than expected?
- Do you need to adjust spending budgets to deal with the good news? Are there some inventories that need beefing up? Changes in production schedules? And with the improved sales results, is there more money available for more spending, to improve results even further?

All you have to do is track the plan vs. actual sales and you can see the management that follows.

Like a business plan, you can measure the value of a sales forecast by measuring the business decisions it causes.

Author Note: This reminds me of a discussion that came up when I was consulting to an international group in a large American company. The manager would first get the middle managers to commit to a sales target and then decrease the marketing budgets. Those middle managers would insist on

By Lisay via istockphoto.com

tying the sales target to the marketing budget, so a decrease in spending meant a corresponding decrease in sales targets. That made sense to all. The point is that the sales forecast doesn't live alone; it manages the company.

And it gets better. Once you have a sales forecast going, and budgets in place, then you have tools to steer your business according to events. Reality rears up. Honestly, sales are always different from the forecast, and that's where the management comes in: If sales are doing better than the original forecast, hooray, you figure out what's working better than planned and do more of it. If sales are less than forecast, you adjust your budgets accordingly, to turn the knobs of the business to correct problems, or, worst case, cut expenses to minimize the hurt.

Think of the sales forecast and the key to knowing what knobs to turn. Well managed, it's like a speedometer, or maybe a GPS.

So that's what this book is about: setting up the initial forecast, whether for new things or existing things, and then following up with plan vs. actual reviews, as well as course corrections, to manage your business.

About Fear of Forecasting

Is math anxiety a real thing? The Google search gets more than half a million hits. And the Google search for "Fear of forecasting," to get more to the point, gets more than 953,000 hits.

Author Note: Can I call that a million? I think so—maybe you'll want to refer to the discussion on rounding in chapter 10. In the meantime, ROUND ("fear of forecasting," –5) = One million. I'll explain that later.

I think there's no need for that fear of forecasting. It comes from the idea that somebody else (or in some cases, everybody else) is more qualified. You assume that the person with the CPA certification, MBA degree, or PhD in statistics is supposed to do forecasting. Not you. You don't have the training.

The truth, however, is that real sales forecasting for actual businesses is almost always a matter of knowing the business, knowing the market, and applying common sense. I do have the fancy MBA, and I did spend my years with a market research firm, and what I learned with that is that you, the entrepreneur, the founder, the manager, or the owner, know more about what's going to happen than any outside expert.

New vs. Existing Business

It's also true that the forecasting is much harder when you're looking at a new business, product, or service. You don't have history. You can't apply that knowledge and experience as easily.

Even in that case, though, it's still not something that experts know and you don't. It's a more difficult educated guess, but it's not like there's an answer out there and you have to find it.

What you're after, in that case, is detailed assumptions. If you feel like glancing ahead at the next chapter you'll see several examples of forecasting for new businesses using detailed assumptions that explain the forecast.

Common Sense and Educated Guessing

I've been dealing with fear or forecasting for normal people in startups and small businesses for more than 30 years now. It seems like the best cure for that fear is to realize that only a very few forecasts are actually based on rigorous market research or sophisticated methodologies. Most of it is common sense and laying out reasonable assumptions.

All Forecasts Are Wrong—But Vital!

It's important to understand that sales forecasting isn't really about being right. You're not going to guess the future correctly, so you can relax. What you want is to record your guess and your assumptions accurately so that when you're wrong—and you will be wrong—you can use that forecasting tracking to go back and review how the forecast linked to sales and marketing programs, other business activities, cash flow, and management.

Author Note: Consider this: hard as it may be to forecast your sales, it's even harder to manage a business without a forecast.

How to Use This Book

Feel free to browse, using the chapter titles. Each chapter could stand alone.

I have to apologize in advance for slipping from "I" to "we" to "you" tones at different times. Sometimes I feel like I'm sharing tips and experience from more than 30 years of sales forecasting; so it feels good to just be me. Then sometimes I'm imagining me and you and others working together doing a forecast, as if we're sitting in the conference room working with the computer projected onto a larger screen. And sometimes it feels like it's just me and you, and I'm talking to you. I hope you don't mind.

There is an underlying logic to the order of chapters. There's this introductory chapter, then a quick see-it's-not-so-hard view of practical forecasting (in chapter 2), then the obligatory information gathering chapter (chapter 3), then a series of specific forecasting types and methods in chapters 4–8. Some of these methods-and-technique-based chapters would cast doubt on my general view that it's all common sense. That's paradox, and it's just a part of business. I can't resolve that for you, but I can hint that the subject is broad enough to withstand both the emphasis on common sense and discussion of a few of the finer points. Then in chapter 9, my personal favorite, although one of the shortest, I get back to the real world of management, discussing how to manage a sales forecast in a business setting.

Chapter 10 is where I collect a lot of the spreadsheet tips and traps. These are things like the real spreadsheet function behind my facetious reference to ROUND up above and compound average growth formulas, useful functions, and so on. I've collected them for you and me in chapter 10 because I do want to cover them, but feel like they break the flow if I go into them while I'm writing about forecasting methods. Also, I think they may be more useful to you when collected in one place.

CHAPTER 2

About Forecasting

Forecasting is more art than science. There are no magic methods that always work, let alone a computer program that will forecast by itself. The heart of forecasting is guessing well, and the best guess is an educated guess. So use your common sense and judgment and as much information as possible. As you prepare a forecast, first look at as many angles as you can, consider past trends, new developments, cycles, and anything else that might give you a hint.

Consider the weather forecast, which is one of the best forecasts available anywhere. Meteorologists study wind patterns, satellite pictures, air pressure, and years of past trends. Each forecast is based on careful analysis of what's going on and why and how it might lead to something else tomorrow. If a storm is over the ocean and headed toward the coast, then they predict rain, because many similar storms produced rain in the past. Their forecasts are professional guesses, based on knowledge, experience, and common sense. Computers, satellites, and other technical tools increase the accuracy of a forecast, but only if they are correctly applied by human judgment.

The same general idea applies to many other types of forecasts. The best forecast combines sophisticated information management with good common sense. Market researchers, stock analysts, and political pundits base their guesses on huge volumes of carefully analyzed information. They might use computerized econometric or simulation models, or complicated trends analysis. But even the most sophisticated computerized forecasting models do a little more than pull equations out of the past and project them into the future. Computer modeling is a very good way to consider alternatives and test assumptions, but there is still no substitute for common sense.

Critical Difference

New Business vs. Past Data

I referred to this problem in the previous chapter. It boils down to a question I get a lot in e-mail: "How could I possibly know? This is a new business (or product or service). I have no data."

The idea behind this question is fundamentally true: It is much easier to do a sales forecast by starting with last year's sales, if you have last year's sales, than almost any other way.

On the other hand, new businesses do get started, and they often forecast their sales before they start. The sales forecast is a critical component of a reasonable business plan. So lots of people get through this problem somehow.

And I intend to show you how they do it. You'll see that in three of the four forecast examples in this chapter, and it comes up again in chapters 5–7.

And in the meantime, I'd add, "Come on, you're hardly the only one. You can still forecast those sales. Just focus more on reasonable assumptions."

Spreadsheets and Forecasting

As you know already if you've read the previous chapter, I'm collecting spreadsheet specifics in chapter 10 at the end of the book. Still, we can't talk about sales forecasting without the language of the spreadsheets, so we do need to cover some basics here before we go further.

Spreadsheets and sales forecasting were made for each other. Sure, there are some more specialized tools, such as statistical analysis and all; but in the real world, entrepreneurs, owners, and managers flock to the spreadsheet for the sales forecast.

So in many ways, the language of forecasting is spreadsheets. Think of that as a phenomenon that started about 30 years ago with Visicalc, followed by Lotus 1–2–3 and a flock of others, which we all now pretty much think of as Microsoft Excel ®.

Rows and Columns

If you're familiar with spreadsheets already, then you'll probably want to skip quickly through this next section. I'm talking about the basics of spreadsheets.

The simple spreadsheet illustration here shows you the basic building blocks of a simple spreadsheet for sales forecasting. Let's start by looking at the basic geography of the spreadsheet.

- The spreadsheet is arranged in rows and columns.
- Rows are horizontal, and numbered from 1 to whatever.
- Columns are vertical, identified by letters from A to whatever. And not just 26 of them. After Z comes AA, and after AZ comes BA, and so on. Forever.
- In sales forecasting, you normally have row labels running down the leftmost column in column A and time frames (months, weeks, quarter, years, etc.) running across the topmost row, in Row 1. That's what you see in the sample in Figure 2.1.
- Cell E5 is selected. That shows in the selection highlight at the upper left. It also shows with the highlighting of row 5 and column E.

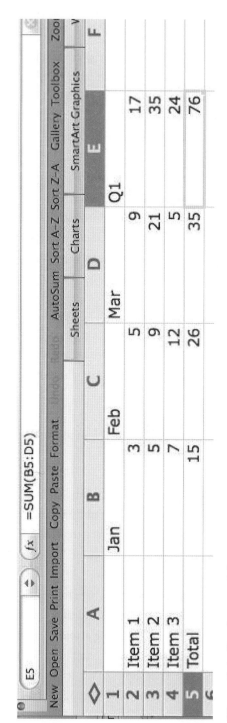

Figure 2.1. Simple spreadsheet.

- The formula applied to cell E5 shows in the edit bar, also called formula bar, along the top, to the right of the selected cell indicator: " = SUM(B5:D5)." That formula applies the sum of the contents of cells B5, C5, and D5 and shows the number in E5. So 15 + 26 + 35 = 76.

From there it doesn't take much imagination to visualize a simple spreadsheet-based sales forecast, as shown in Figure 2.2. Please don't be taken aback by the size, because when you take it step by step, this is really simple. Bear with me as you take your first look, then let's go over the explanation below the illustration.

You need to extend your imagination a bit, beyond the constraints of page size, to see the whole spreadsheet.

- It starts with row labels, as we call them, in column A. You can see what that means if you look at the illustration. "Sales Forecast," for example, in Cell A1, is a row label. It's just a small text explaining what's there. You can also see here how the labels repeat from units, to price, to sales, to unit costs, to costs. For "Lunches," for example, you see the same labels in row 11, 17, 24, 36, and 30. I hope you can see why.
- Columns D–K are hidden, for this illustration, because of the limits of page width. Hiding a column is a simple spreadsheet feature. They're still there, though, and still calculating.
- There are 12 columns, B–M, used for calculating the first 12 months of the forecast.
- Column N calculates the total for the first year of the forecast (2010) by adding up the totals from the 12 months. For example, you can see in the edit bar at the top of the illustration that the formula for cell N4 is

$$= SUM(C19{:}N19)$$

and it displays the result, which is 3,594.

| N4 | ▾ | f_x | =SUM(B4:M4) |

	A	B	C	...	L	M	N	O	P
1	**Sales Forecast**	Jan	Feb	Nov	Dec	2010	2011	2012
2									
3	**Unit Sales**								
4	Lunches	200	220	403	443	3,594	4,800	5,200
5	Dinners	450	473	608	638	6,466	9,000	11,000
6	Drinks	488	520	758	811	7,546	10,350	12,150
7	Other	50	60	150	160	1,260	1,500	1,750
8	**Total Unit Sales**	1,188	1,273	1,919	2,052	18,866	25,650	30,100
9									
10	**Unit Prices**	Jan	Feb	Nov	Dec	2010	2011	2012
11	Lunches	$7.00	$7.00	$7.00	$7.00	$7.00	$7.00	$7.00
12	Dinners	$14.50	$14.50	$14.50	$14.50	$14.50	$14.50	$14.50
13	Drinks	$3.50	$3.50	$3.50	$3.50	$3.50	$3.50	$3.50
14	Other	$15.00	$15.00	$15.00	$15.00	$15.00	$15.00	$15.00
15									
16	**Sales**								
17	Lunches	$1,400	$1,540	$2,821	$3,101	$25,158	$33,600	$36,400
18	Dinners	$6,525	$6,859	$8,816	$9,251	$93,757	$130,500	$159,500
19	Drinks	$1,708	$1,820	$2,653	$2,839	$26,411	$36,225	$42,525
20	Other	$750	$900	$2,250	$2,400	$18,900	$22,500	$26,250
21	**Total Sales**	$10,383	$11,119	$16,540	$17,591	$164,226	$222,825	$264,675

Figure 2.2. Simple sales forecast.

- Column N has to be careful with what it does with the unit prices. I'll have more about that later, chapter 10, under spreadsheet fine points.
- Rows 8, 21, and 34 sum down the columns in another simple and obvious variation on spreadsheet summing formulas. Can you guess the formula for cell C8? If you guessed

$$= SUM(C4:C7),$$

then you guessed right.

Some Simple Refinements

I hope you see that the basic math and spreadsheet logic is pretty simple. The truth is that the real hard part of forecasting is making that educated guess, not doing the math. And believe me, we will deal—later—with how you fill those rows with the assumptions they have. But for now, more on the mechanics.

	N12	f_x	=IF(N5<>0,N18/N5,0)	
	A	M	N	O
1	Sales Forecast			
2		Dec	2010	2011
3	Unit Sales			
4	Lunches	443	3,594	4,800
5	Dinners	638	6,466	9,000
6	Drinks	811	7,546	10,350
7	Other	160	1,260	1,500
8	Total Unit Sales	2,052	18,866	25,650
9				
10	Unit Prices	Dec	2010	2011
11	Lunches	$7.00	$7.00	$7.00
12	Dinners	$14.50	$14.50	$14.50
13	Drinks	$3.50	$3.50	$3.50

Figure 2.3. Average prices.

Consider the formula I used here for calculating the annual value for unit price. The temptation is to take the average of the dinner price entries for the year, which in this case is just $14.50 (because as it turns out, in this sales forecast, there is a steady and unchanging price). But what if the prices have been changing? Will adding up the average for the 12 months, then dividing by 12, give you the average price? No. What if you sold only 50 dinners in January for $10.00, but 200 dinners in February for $15.00? The average of the two monthly dinner price cells would be $12.50; but the average price would be $14.00 *(because 10 + 15 is 25, which, when divided by 2, is 12.5; but 500 + 3,000 is 3,500, which, divided by 250, is 14).*

The best forecasting takes many different possibilities into account. Good forecasters consider many different assumptions. They put them up on the spreadsheet screen and think about them. Eventually they go with one analysis or another, or absorb all the numbers and estimate some in between.

There is more about this price averaging problem in chapter 10, on spreadsheet fine points. And that discussion covers the "=IF" logic too.

Breaking the Forecast Into Pieces

One of the least understood elements of forecasting is the need for breaking simple assumptions into pieces. You lay them out so you can see them. That also makes things easier to explain.

For example, in the world of business planning for new businesses, people tend to think of forecasts as being validated by daunting and expensive market research; in truth, however, it's much more likely to be a matter of documenting assumptions. You make assumptions visible so somebody else can understand them.

More on Spreadsheets in Chapter 10

I've left a lot of finer points about spreadsheets and forecasting for chapter 9. Here we focus on the absolute essentials. In chapter 10, we look at refining some formulas, IF clauses, spreadsheet logic, and other additional tips.

Simple Is Better: Some Case Examples

The New Restaurant, Case 1

To show how sales forecasting for a new business can lever off common sense instead of research, I'd like to share an example built for a new restaurant. Let's take the case of Magda and her new restaurant.

Magda was looking at forecasting sales for a small restaurant. Her problem wasn't finding some magic number in market research, or an answer on the Web hidden like a pot of gold at the end of the rainbow. It was how to develop a sales forecast she could believe in, explain, and manage with. She needed some way to build a forecast on reasonable assumptions. So here is what she did.

She focused on her location. She decided she would be able to seat six tables of four people each as a starting point. She knew that things might change when she actually decided on the space to rent, but she had to start somewhere, so six tables of four it was. That comes to look like what you see here in Figure 2.4.

Then she did some simple math: six tables of four meant at capacity she would be serving 24 meals. Meals take about an hour at lunch, and about 2 hours at dinner. She figured she'd have one serving of lunch and two of dinner, roughly calculating the 5 to 5:30 crowd as the first serving and the

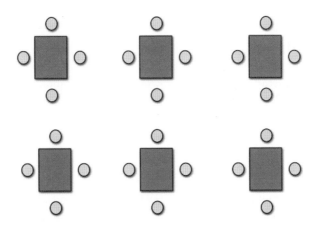

Figure 2.4. Tables and chairs.

By c via Shutterstock

7:30 to 8 crowd as the second serving. So an absolutely full lunch service in a day would be 24 lunches. An absolutely full dinner service in a day would be 48 dinners.

So here is some math:

1. 6 tables × people per table = 24 people.
2. 24 people × 1 lunch = 24 lunches at capacity.
3. 24 lunches × 21 work days = 504 lunches at capacity.
4. 24 people × 2 = 48 dinners at capacity.
5. 48 dinners × 26 dinner days = 1,248 dinners monthly at capacity.

So for a theoretical full capacity month, Magda would be serving approximately 500 lunches and 1,250 dinners (taken from 504 and 1,248 in the list above; rounding numbers makes it clear they are guesses, while leaving them at 504 and 1,248 would give the false impression of exactness and specificity).

Magda takes that math as establishing general parameters, and then she thinks through the realities of getting opened, startup marketing, and promotion, to come up with a sales forecast showing about 40% of capacity in lunches and slightly less in dinners for the first month, then gradually increasing. A partial view of that is in Figure 2.5. Notice that this is very similar to the one in Figure 2.2; but Magda has inserted a new column B, moving the other columns to the right, to allow for some assumptions.

She uses the assumptions with simple spreadsheet formulas:

- The forecast for lunches is growing at 10% per month. The formula for cell D19, lunches in February, to show one example, is

$$= ROUND(C19 * (1 + \$B\$19),0),$$

  which multiplies the 200 in C19 by 1.1 and rounds that to the nearest whole number (please bear with me for now on the use of $ to show absolute references and the rounding functions, which I've left for Spreadsheet Fine Points in chapter 10. To explain them here would break up the flow).

	A	B	C	D	E	F
			Jan	Feb	Mar	Apr
16	**Sales Forecast**					
17						
18	**Unit Sales**					
19	Lunches	10%	200	220	242	266
20	Dinners	5%	450	473	497	522
21	Drinks	75%	488	520	554	591
22	Other		50	60	70	80
23	**Total Unit Sales**		1,188	1,273	1,363	1,459
24						
25	**Unit Prices**		Jan	Feb	Mar	Apr
26	Lunches		$7.00	$7.00	$7.00	$7.00
27	Dinners		$14.50	$14.50	$14.50	$14.50
28	Drinks		$3.50	$3.50	$3.50	$3.50
29	Other		$15.00	$15.00	$15.00	$15.00
30						
31	**Sales**					
32	Lunches		$1,400	$1,540	$1,694	$1,862
33	Dinners		$6,525	$6,859	$7,207	$7,569
34	Drinks		$1,706	$1,820	$1,939	$2,069
35	Other		$750	$900	$1,050	$1,200
36	**Total Sales**		$10,381	$11,119	$11,890	$12,700

Figure 2.5. Simple sample sales forecast.

- The forecast for dinners is growing at 5% per month.
- Drinks are set with a simple spreadsheet formula that assumes 75% of the meals include one drink. That's just an average. It's an assumption. The formula for cell C21, drinks in January, is

$$= ROUND(\$B\$21 * (C19 + C20),0).$$

So now consider what Magda has gained. No, she doesn't have market research to prove or validate her educated guess for the early months of her restaurant. She does, however, have visible assumptions that she can explain. She has a basis for forecasting lunches, dinners, drinks, and other sales (t-shirts). If she needs to discuss her forecast with an investor or partner or significant other, there is a rationale behind it.

And as we fill in the rest of the assumptions, to create the sales forecast we see in Figure 2.6, you can see how what seems like a large and daunting sales forecast is actually a matter of building up with blocks.

If you look carefully, you'll see that Magda has also built (using the spreadsheet) reasonable assumptions to determine her direct cost of sales:

- Magda added seasonality to fine-tune her monthly meals estimates. The smooth monthly growth assumptions break in June and July when the estimate goes down. We call that seasonality.
- The average lunch costs her 25% of the $7.00 average price she charges. That's her estimate for the foodstuffs in the meal—what she pays to buy the meat and bread and potatoes and so on.
- The average dinner costs 25% as well.
- The average drink costs her 15%. That's the soft drink syrup, or the beer or wine bottles she serves.
- And the average "other" (t-shirts) costs her 35% of what she charges.

You can also see how we put all of this together in the forecast. Detail by detail, we build on assumptions and explain. The units assumptions multiplied by price assumptions create the actual sales estimates. And the units assumptions multiplied by the cost per unit assumptions create the direct costs estimates.

	A	B	C	D	M	N	O	P	Q
1	Sales Forecast								
2			Jan	Feb	Nov	Dec	2010	2011	2012
3	Unit Sales								
4	Lunches	10%	200	220	403	443	3,594	4,800	5,200
5	Dinners	5%	450	473	608	638	6,466	9,000	11,000
6	Drinks	75%	488	520	758	811	7,545	10,350	12,150
7	Other		50	60	150	160	1,260	1,500	1,750
8	Total Unit Sales		1,188	1,273	1,919	2,052	18,865	25,650	30,100
9									
10	Unit Prices		Jan	Feb	Nov	Dec	2010	2011	2012
11	Lunches		$7.00	$7.00	$7.00	$7.00	$7.00	$7.00	$7.00
12	Dinners		$14.50	$14.50	$14.50	$14.50	$14.50	$14.50	$14.50
13	Drinks		$3.50	$3.50	$3.50	$3.50	$3.50	$3.50	$3.50
14	Other		$15.00	$15.00	$15.00	$15.00	$15.00	$15.00	$15.00
15									
16	Sales								
17	Lunches		$1,400	$1,540	$2,821	$3,101	$25,158	$33,600	$36,400
18	Dinners		$6,525	$6,859	$8,816	$9,251	$93,757	$130,500	$159,500
19	Drinks		$1,706	$1,820	$2,653	$2,839	$26,409	$36,227	$42,528
20	Other		$750	$900	$2,250	$2,400	$18,900	$22,500	$26,250
21	Total Sales		$10,381	$11,119	$16,540	$17,591	$164,224	$222,827	$264,678
22									
23	Direct Unit Costs		Jan	Feb	Nov	Dec	2010	2011	2012
24	Lunches	25.00%	$1.75	$1.75	$1.75	$1.75	$1.75	$1.75	$1.75
25	Dinners	25.00%	$3.63	$3.63	$3.63	$3.63	$3.63	$3.63	$3.63
26	Drinks	15.00%	$0.53	$0.53	$0.53	$0.53	$0.53	$0.53	$0.53
27	Other	35.00%	$5.25	$5.25	$5.25	$5.25	$5.25	$5.25	$5.25
28									
29	Direct Cost of Sales								
30	Lunches		$350	$385	$705	$775	$6,290	$8,400	$9,100
31	Dinners		$1,631	$1,715	$2,204	$2,313	$23,439	$32,625	$39,875
32	Drinks		$256	$273	$398	$426	$3,961	$5,434	$6,379
33	Other		$263	$315	$788	$840	$6,615	$7,875	$9,188
34	Subtotal Direct Cost of Sales		$2,500	$2,687	$4,095	$4,354	$40,305	$54,334	$64,541

Figure 2.6. The complete sample sales forecast.

And there we have it: a sales forecast for a new business, based on reasonable and explainable assumptions. Piece by piece, we built it from the bricks.

Author Note: And here we should add what really happens when we have actual entrepreneurship and good management: By the third week in February, Magda will be comparing her actual sales results to the planned sales, analyzing the difference, adjusting her expense budgets as well as her sales forecast, and using that forecast and the actual results to make a better business out of it.

Second Example: Simple Restaurant, Case 2

This kind of forecasting is not a matter of academic background or magic answers somebody learned in some school somewhere. It's common sense. With that in mind, let's look at an alternative scenario for Magda's restaurant.

In this second case, Magda realizes that she's better off focusing on a higher-end customer and differentiating with a slightly higher price. The high price says better food and better service. She has rented a locale that will lend itself to that slightly revised strategy, so she wants to revise her forecast. She's also decided to increase her financing. She's spending a bit more to fix the place up, to make it match the higher price strategy.

Author Note: *The forecast doesn't happen in a vacuum: It's closely related to strategy and resources available to support it.*

Figure 2.7 shows a second set of assumptions for Magda's second-take forecast. She's added more detail.

This time around, Magda looks at capacity in terms of meals and drinks for different days of the week, in an average month. Friday night dinners are much more likely to be full than Monday night dinners. There are no lunches at all for Saturday and Sunday.

She's also revised her pricing. Both lunches and dinners are more expensive in this second scenario than in the first. And she's decided to project drinks at lunch and at dinner as separate rows in the forecast. Dinner drinks are more likely to be more expensive. The result is the forecast in Figure 2.8.

Which of the two forecasts is better? Time will tell. The higher price seems well suited to the location and the strategy. And breaking the beverages down into two separate rows makes it easier to track plan vs. actual later on, which is vital. That's where most of the business value comes.

And the second forecast has higher sales, too.

Third Example: Web-Traffic-Based Forecast

Again, this is just hypothetical, but can be useful as an example. Another good way to anchor a forecast with assumptions is to look at the built-in link between Web marketing spending, Web search engine placement, Web traffic, conversion rates, and sales. Take this sample forecast in Figure 2.9.

This forecast continues like the others, with direct cost of sales per unit and total direct cost of sales below the rows shown and with the rest

| K31 | | f_x | =ROUND((J31*52)/12, 0) | | | | | | | |

	A	B	C	D	E	F	G	H	I	J	K
19	Units	Capacity	Sun	Mon	Tues	Wed	Thurs	Fri	Sat	Total	Baseline month
20	Lunch	24	0	14	16	18	18	20	0	86	373
21	lunch beverage	24	0	14	16	18	18	20	0	86	373
22	Dinner	48	35	22	28	30	30	48	48	241	1,044
23	Dinner beverage	48	35	22	28	30	30	48	48	241	1,044
24	Total	144	70	72	88	96	96	136	96	654	2,834
25	Unit prices										
26	Lunch		$10.00	$10.00	$10.00	$10.00	$10.00	$10.00	$10.00		
27	lunch beverage		$2.00	$2.00	$2.00	$2.00	$2.00	$2.00	$2.00		
28	Dinner		$20.00	$20.00	$20.00	$20.00	$20.00	$20.00	$20.00		
29	Dinner beverage		$4.00	$4.00	$4.00	$4.00	$4.00	$4.00	$4.00		
30	Sales										
31	Lunch		$0	$140	$160	$180	$180	$200	$0	$860	$3,727
32	lunch beverage		$0	$28	$32	$36	$36	$40	$0	$172	$745
33	Dinner		$700	$440	$560	$600	$600	$960	$960	$4,820	$20,887
34	Dinner beverage		$140	$88	$112	$120	$120	$192	$192	$964	$4,177
35	Total		$840	$696	$864	$936	$936	$1,392	$1,152	$6,816	$29,536

Figure 2.7. Second set of assumptions.

E34	=E19*E27					
	A		C	D	E	F
16	**Sales Forecast**					
17			Jan	Feb	Mar	Apr
18	**Unit Sales**					
19	Lunches		119	227	302	326
20	Lunch Bvg		119	227	302	326
21	Dinners		500	600	728	652
22	Dinner Bvg		500	454	604	652
23	Other		50	83	103	98
24	**Total Unit Sales**		1,288	1,591	2,039	2,054
25						
26	**Unit Prices**		Jan	Feb	Mar	Apr
27	Lunches		$10.00	$10.00	$10.00	$10.00
28	Lunch Bvg		$2.00	$2.00	$2.00	$2.00
29	Dinners		$20.00	$20.00	$20.00	$20.00
30	Dinner Bvg		$4.00	$4.00	$4.00	$4.00
31	Other		$10.00	$10.00	$10.00	$10.00
32						
33	**Sales**					
34	Lunches		$1,190	$2,270	$3,020	$3,260
35	Lunch Bvg		$238	$454	$604	$652
36	Dinners		$10,000	$12,000	$14,560	$13,040
37	Dinner Bvg		$2,000	$1,816	$2,416	$2,608
38	Other		$500	$830	$1,030	$980
39	**Total Sales**		$13,928	$17,370	$21,630	$20,540
40						

Figure 2.8. Second forecast.

F9	=ROUND($B$9*F7,-1)						
	A	B	C	D	E	F	G
1	**Sales Forecast**						
2			Jan	Feb	Mar	Apr	May
3	**Web Traffic**						
4	Organic	0%	2,000	7,000	8,000	9,000	9,000
5	PPC Clicks	0%	8,000	19,403	25,622	28,358	33,084
6	Other	1%	100	264	336	374	421
7	**Total Unique Visitors**		10,100	26,667	33,958	37,732	42,505
8							
9	Conversion	1%	0	0	340	380	430
10	PPC cost	$1.15	$9,200	$22,313	$29,465	$32,612	$38,047
11							
12	**Unit Sales**						
13	Toys and Games	0%	0	0	340	380	430
14	Books	0%	0	0	0	40	40
15	Software	0%	0	0	0	80	90
16	**Total Unit Sales**		0	0	1,194	2,527	3,674
17							
18	**Unit Prices**		Jan	Feb	Mar	Apr	May
19	Toys and Games		$30.00	$30.00	$30.00	$30.00	$30.00
20	Books		$20.00	$20.00	$20.00	$20.00	$20.00
21	Software		$40.00	$40.00	$40.00	$40.00	$40.00
22							
23	**Sales**						
24	Toys and Games		$0	$0	$35,820	$68,670	$97,011
25	Books		$0	$0	$0	$2,687	$5,373
26	Software		$0	$0	$0	$4,160	$6,880
27	**Total Sales**		$0	$0	$35,820	$75,517	$109,265

Figure 2.9. Web-traffic-based forecast.

of the year and years 2012 and 2013 to the right, not shown because of the constraints of page size.

What you do see here is a clearly laid out set of assumptions about unique visitors, conversions, and Web search term pay-per-click expenses. The unique visitors are set as a combination of organic traffic, search term pay-per-click traffic, conversion rate, and expenses of the pay-per-click traffic at an estimated $1.15 per click.

Author Note: If you have no idea what any of that means, you probably aren't involved in a startup Web business. If you are, and you have no idea, then you have some homework. This book is about the sales forecasting elements, not the Web marketing.

What we see here is another simple and logical forecast whose assumptions generate the detail of the forecast. For the record, it is an extremely optimistic projection of starting Web traffic. In the real world, this startup company would have to have some powerful marketing budgets to generate traffic that fast.

As it is, you can see here that the pay-per-click budget is substantial: Beyond $20,000 per month by the second month and almost $40,000 by the fifth. The good news, though, is that if the assumptions hold up, sales are higher than pay-per-click expenses.

Fourth Example: Projecting Next Year From This Year

A local computer business is developing a sales forecast to go along with its business plan for the next year. Its sales are divided into five general sales rows, as you see in Figure 2.10.

Author Note: Of course this computer business has hundreds and maybe thousands of stock-keeping units (SKUs) for its inventory. But for sales forecasting, we need to simplify the assumptions. It's planning, not accounting. You can't pretend to forecast by specific SKU for hundreds of SKUs. You need to aggregate and summarize).

So what we want to do with this is project the sales for each of these product lines for the coming year. We're not going to go out and do complex market research, but we are going to study our market prospects, threats and opportunities, and work interactively with our business plan.

	A	B	C	D	E
1	**2010 Actual Sales**				
2		**Jan-10**	**Feb-10**	**Mar-10**	**Apr-10**
3	**Unit Sales**				
4	Systems	52	78	110	148
5	Service	106	104	116	143
6	Software	43	56	65	89
7	Training	103	113	113	123
8	Other	126	139	154	183
9	**Total Unit Sales**	430	490	558	686
10					
11	**Unit Prices**	Jan	Feb	Mar	Apr
12	Systems	$1,800.00	$1,764.00	$1,728.72	$1,694.15
13	Service	$75.00	$75.75	$76.51	$77.28
14	Software	$96.30	$85.60	$102.21	$94.71
15	Training	$37.00	$37.00	$37.00	$37.00
16	Other	$263.61	$269.05	$251.15	$264.25
17					
18	**Sales**				
19	Systems	$93,600	$137,592	$190,159	$250,734
20	Service	$7,950	$7,878	$8,875	$11,051
21	Software	$4,141	$4,794	$6,644	$8,429
22	Training	$3,811	$4,181	$4,181	$4,551
23	Other	$33,215	$37,398	$38,677	$48,358
24	**Total Sales**	$142,717	$191,843	$248,536	$323,123
25					
26	**Direct Unit Costs**	Jan	Feb	Mar	Apr
27	Systems	$1,530.00	$1,499.40	$1,469.41	$1,440.03
28	Service	$30.00	$30.00	$30.00	$30.00
29	Software	$120.00	$120.00	$120.00	$120.00
30	Training	$11.10	$11.10	$11.10	$11.10
31	Other	$90.00	$90.00	$90.00	$90.00
32					
33	**Total Costs**				
34	Systems	$79,560	$116,953	$161,635	$213,124
35	Service	$3,180	$3,120	$3,480	$4,290
36	Software	$5,160	$6,720	$7,800	$10,680
37	Training	$1,143	$1,254	$1,254	$1,365
38	Other	$11,340	$12,510	$13,860	$16,470
39	**Direct Cost Total**	$100,383	$140,558	$188,030	$245,929
40					

Figure 2.10. Organized actual sales for current year.

We need to deal with trends. One of the good shortcuts is to put the trends onto a visual, so we can absorb them more quickly. I like a simple line chart, like the one in Figure 2.11, showing unit sales for each of the five categories in the current year.

So what we see there is a generally favorable trend and some guesses to explore. It looks like software seems to go way up at the end of the year but down in the summer. That generates questions. Talk to managers. What happened? Did we have special promotions, or special market situations? Can we repeat the growth in the spring, and avoid the dive in summer? Service units seem to rise steadily: why? Training is more stable but growing. What does this tell us about the next year?

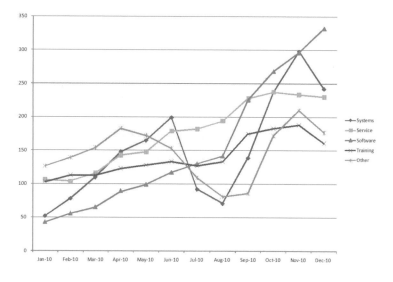

Figure 2.11. Line chart of current sales.

A lot of the reality of a business plan forecast like this one doesn't show in the chart. It's the talking with the managers, the experience of the current year. And also the strategy, like where are we going to put more emphasis in the coming year? Where is there more money to be spent and why? What has worked in the current year, and what are we changing in the coming year?

Author Note: There's a theme here. Real business forecasting is based much more on plans and recent results than outside formal market research. Don't ever fail to forecast because you don't have time or budget for research. Talk to people instead. Talk to your managers and your customers.

So how can we make sense of the multiline chart above and develop a forecast? After a lot of discussion, analysis, and planning, we take one line of sales at a time and develop a forecast, extrapolating last year and adding in our specific plans to create an estimated guess for next year. Figure 2.12 shows our sales of systems units in the current year.

The pattern is pretty clear from the chart. It drops in summer, and drops again in December. Managers will discuss what business activities helped to foster the growth in the good months, and what might

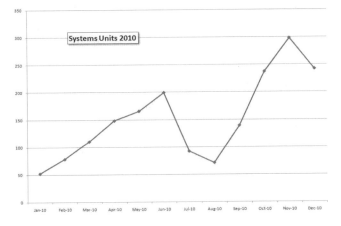

Figure 2.12. Systems units current year.

be involved in the big drops. That's not really forecasting; that's called management and business planning.

So what's the plan for next year? The 2011 project comes in Figure 2.13, compared to 2010. You can see in that chart that the business plan looks to repeat the big growth in spring, and reduce somewhat the drop-off in the summer. It's not magic.

Author Note: Sales forecasts have to be as realistic as possible. Wishful thinking does you no good. Don't think a sales forecast that's too high will pull sales up along with it. It just discourages management, and bogs people down with unrealistic expectations.

I won't take you through the same routine for the other four sales lines, but you can imagine. One by one, there's a consideration of past results and future plans, realism, and eventually, a sales projection.

When it's done, you can project a 24-month view of the sales by line, in a line chart showing the current year's actual results and the forecast for the next year. That's shown in Figure 2.14.

And, ultimately, the sales forecast. That's in Figure 2.15.

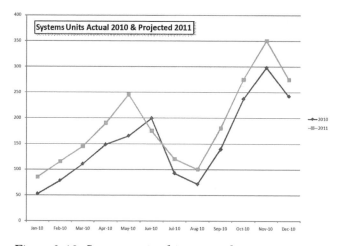

Figure 2.13. Systems units this year and next.

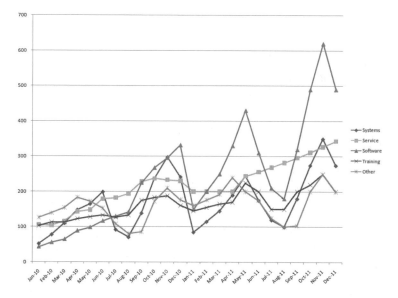

Figure 2.14. The two-year projection.

	A	N	O	P	~	X	Y	Z	AA	AB
1	**Sales Forecast**									
2		Jan-11	Feb-11	Mar-11		Nov-11	Dec-11	2011	2012	2013
3	**Unit Sales**									
4	Systems	85	115	145		350	275	2,255	2,500	2,800
5	Service	200	200	200		327	343	3,128	4,000	5,000
6	Software	150	200	250		620	490	3,980	5,000	6,500
7	Training	145	155	165		250	200	2,230	4,000	8,000
8	Other	160	176	192		250	200	2,122	2,500	3,000
9	**Total Unit Sales**	740	846	952		1,797	1,508	13,715	18,000	25,300
10										
11	**Unit Prices**	Jan	Feb	Mar		Nov	Dec	2011	2012	2013
12	Systems	$1,412.50	$1,384.25	$1,356.57	$1,	$1,154.13	$1,131.05	$1,241.29	$1,100.00	$1,000.00
13	Service	$90.00	$90.90	$91.81		$99.43	$100.42	$95.75	$100.00	$110.00
14	Software	$84.83	$84.83	$84.83		$84.83	$84.83	$84.83	$195.00	$180.00
15	Training	$37.00	$37.00	$37.00		$37.00	$37.00	$37.00	$45.00	$55.00
16	Other	$283.43	$286.26	$289.12	$	$313.08	$316.21	$299.65	$375.00	$400.00
17										
18	**Sales**									
19	Systems	$120,063	$159,189	$196,703	$25	$403,946	$311,039	$2,799,111	$2,750,000	$2,800,000
20	Service	$18,000	$18,180	$18,362	$18	$32,514	$34,444	$299,507	$400,000	$550,000
21	Software	$12,725	$16,966	$21,208	$	$52,595	$41,567	$337,623	$975,000	$1,170,000
22	Training	$5,365	$5,735	$6,105		$9,250	$7,400	$82,510	$180,000	$440,000
23	Other	$45,349	$50,382	$55,511		$78,270	$63,242	$635,860	$937,500	$1,200,000
24	**Total Sales**	$201,501	$250,452	$297,888	$3	$576,574	$457,692	$4,154,612	$5,242,500	$6,160,000
25										
26	**Direct Unit Costs**	Jan	Feb	Mar		Nov	Dec	2011	2012	2013
27	Systems	$1,200.63	$1,176.61	$1,153.08	$	$981.01	$961.39	$1,055.10	$935.00	$850.00
28	Service	$30.00	$30.00	$30.00		$30.00	$30.00	$30.00	$35.00	$40.00
29	Software	$120.00	$120.00	$120.00	$	$120.00	$120.00	$120.00	$120.00	$120.00
30	Training	$11.10	$11.10	$11.10		$11.10	$11.10	$11.10	$11.10	$11.10
31	Other	$90.00	$90.00	$90.00	$	$90.00	$90.00	$90.00	$90.00	$90.00
32										
33	**Total Costs**									
34	Systems	$102,053	$135,310	$167,197	$2	$343,354	$264,383	$2,379,244	$2,337,500	$2,380,000
35	Service	$6,000	$6,000	$6,000	$	$9,810	$10,290	$93,840	$140,000	$200,000
36	Software	$18,000	$24,000	$30,000	$	$74,400	$58,800	$477,600	$600,000	$780,000
37	Training	$1,610	$1,721	$1,832		$2,775	$2,220	$24,753	$44,400	$88,800
38	Other	$14,400	$15,840	$17,280	$	$22,500	$18,000	$190,980	$225,000	$270,000
39	**Direct Cost Total**	$142,063	$182,871	$222,309	$	$452,839	$353,693	$3,166,417	$3,346,900	$3,718,800

Figure 2.15. Resulting sales forecast.

General Comments

It's Still Just Educated Guessing

Sales forecasting with a spreadsheet is, at its best, a good combination of computing power and common-sense judgment. Make some assumptions and then test them for logic and reasonableness. Look at the spreadsheet numbers and look at a graph of the forecast, try different assumptions, do it again and again until you feel comfortable with your forecast and the assumptions it's built on. Also called scenario analysis, this is one of the best ways to consider future alternatives and their implications. Use it in preparing your forecast.

Use the spreadsheet to play with your guesses. Put a guess on the screen and look at it. Try another angle, a different growth rate, and think about it. Use the spreadsheet to set highs and lows and draw out a forecast. The computer can help by speeding up the process.

Break It Into Pieces

Whenever possible, you should take your forecast and break it down into components. Magda looked at meals, drinks, times of day, chairs, and tables. Every forecast in this chapter and, in fact, every one in this book breaks sales into units times price and direct costs into units times direct cost per unit.

Since your forecast will be wrong (as I said in the previous chapter) but vital as you track how it was wrong, in what direction, and so on, then the breaking it down into components will be that much more valuable. Are sales higher than planned because of more unit sales, or higher average prices? Was it a matter of lunch, dinner, or drinks? If the Web forecast is too optimistic, so actual sales are lower than planned, you should be asking did the conversion rate hold up and the traffic disappoint, or was the traffic fine but the conversion was weak.

Always think of it as a matter of divide and conquer. If you break the forecast down into pieces you get two benefits: First, it's easier to do because it's easier to think about each piece rather than the forecast as a whole. Second, it's easier to track and analyze later.

Graphics Can Help a Lot

I wish I had rigorous academic data to prove it, but I am convinced that normal humans can deal with numbers better as pictures (like in Figures 2.11, 2.12, and 2.13) than as just numbers.

I like to do this with spreadsheets: Put the numbers into a chart like one of those in those illustrations, to consider how they look. You can see the forecasting power in Figure 2.12, where we have one sales line showing for two years, one over the other.

Author Note: Not that rigorous academic data ever really proved anything.

Author Note: Quality of information counts much more than the quality of numerical analysis. And quantity of numerical analysis is least important.

Seasonality

You may or may not have heard the word seasonality before. It can make a huge difference in sales forecasts. It's a reference to the fact that lots of businesses are affected by time of the year: Toys sell better in December and beach towels in June. Sometimes it isn't as obvious as those two examples but just as important.

For example, you can see a lot of seasonality in the computer business in Figures 2.11 through 2.15. Sales go way down in the summer and down in December. Whatever the reasons for that might be, I've been involved in a computer business since the early 1980s and I've consulted for dozens of computer stores. That's the way that business goes.

We have a lot of seasonality in Palo Alto Software, the company I founded, where I'm still president as I write this. We sell business planning software. In the 15 years since we first introduced our main product, Business Plan Pro, we've seen sales go up every January, then down again in May, more down through the summer, then back up in September through November, then down in December. It happens every year.

Seasonality will show up in the past data. If it's there, pay attention to it. You can see in this chapter how much it affected that fourth forecasting example. Even in a new business forecast, try to think about how sales might depend on weather, or holidays, or traveling and vacations. If you can, ask somebody already in the business about it.

The Power of Assumptions Laid Out Plainly

I'd like to point out at this point that as I've grown older I've gone from developer of forecasts to reader, user, and critic of forecasts. I read more than a hundred business plans in depth every year. In a normal year I'm a business plan contest judge for the Forbes.com national business plan contest and business plan contests sponsored by Rice University, the University of Texas, and the University of Oregon. Much more important than that, I'm a member of the Willamette Angel Conference, meaning that I put money into an investment fund and vote on the startup company that the fund chooses to invest in. So I'm looking at sales forecasts as a business planning expert, business plan contest judge, and investor.

I bother you with that background because I want to point out that sales forecast assumptions laid out plainly, when they make sense, can provide much greater credibility for a plan than the expert forecast for a large industry or general trend.

I will always feel better about something like Magda's detailed assumptions than I would if she just cited some vague statistic about how many billions of dollars are spent on restaurants and how that number is growing at some percentage. Or about the Web forecast based on search engine spending, traffic projections, and conversion rates.

For a new business, if you're looking to validate a sales forecast, get into the detailed assumptions. Forget the huge sweeping industry generalizations.

CHAPTER 3

Educating Your Guesses

If you're reading this in page order instead of just flipping pages and browsing, then you and I have a problem of paradox. I just finished, at the end of the last chapter, dismissing the big general market forecast as a validator of a sales forecast. I pretty much pushed using detailed assumptions instead, rather than looking for the answer as if it were a pot of gold at the end of the rainbow.

And here we are at this chapter, about gathering information. That seems like a contradiction to me. The way I reconcile those two seemingly opposing views is to remind myself that I use the weather forecast metaphor, and a good weather forecaster wants as much general data about winds and waters and past history as possible, before she makes that prediction for tomorrow.

You gather the data. Just don't believe it.

By Chris Tennant via Shutterstock

A World of Information Surplus

It used to be that information was scarce, and good information was worth a lot of money. When I was a market researcher for Creative Strategies, back in the early 1980s, big companies paid tens of thousands of dollars for good research—even for secondary research, studying what was published.

And while companies still pay lots of money for research today, the nature of the world of information has changed. It's no longer about finding information; no, it's now about making sense of all the information that's available. Or sifting through it all, finding, among all the information available, what part of it is valid and applicable to the problem at hand.

It used to be about finding needles in haystacks. Now it's about finding the right needles in mountains of needles.

Start Simple

According to Wikipedia, *Occam's razor* or *Ockham's razor* is the principle that "entities should not be multiplied unnecessarily" or, popularly applied, "when you have two competing theories that make exactly the same predictions, the simpler one is the better."

For sales forecasting, Occam's razor is a good reminder. Too often we burden sales forecasting with sophisticated economic models and heavy

By Microcozm via istockphoto.com

expensive research: surveys, polls, focus groups, and large budgets. While we do talk about some of those techniques in this book, toward the end, never lose sight of what's right in front of you. Simple is better.

Without a Doubt, Recent Past Is the Best Predictor

Whenever you can, start with last year's sales and extrapolate them forward for the next year.

As you do that, take a few steps away from the business and look at what might be different. Why would sales next year be different from this year? And here too, start with the simple and obvious:

- A lot of businesses have a good general feel for progress and change.
- Is this a growing business with new products and new customers?
- Or is it a mature business, with some products and sales declining?
- It's not often all that scientific. If you've been in business for a while, you have a pretty good sense of how things are going. What we're after is writing it down as a forecast so you can break it into pieces and follow it up with steering and management.

Look at the Line Charts

Consider Figure 3.1, a line chart showing sales from the previous year for a sample business. Drawing the line chart is a simple spreadsheet exercise; we're not going to go into this much spreadsheet detail in this book but it's not hard. Depending on which spreadsheet you're using, it's usually a matter of a few clicks.

Assume you got the data for this from the most recent year. What can you tell about a reasonable forecast for the next year?

You can probably tell a lot. Without knowing anything more than what happened last year, there are several things we can assume about next year. For example

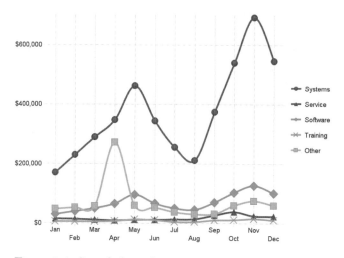

Figure 3.1. Sample line chart.

- You can see some built-in seasonality in this chart. Sales are likely to grow from January through May, then decline into August, then grow again in the fall but decline for December. Of course you season that data with thought and common sense. You ask yourself how much of this was related to one-time phenomena and how much would be a general flow through the year.
- You would probably assume sales of systems are growing, and sales of training are stagnant at best, maybe declining.
- You'd probably assume that sales of systems will be more than double those of software—but you'd ask yourself whether the drop-off of systems sales in December was just a seasonal drop, or something else. You'd want to think about this question, and look for answers.
- You'd also want to see what happened to "Other" sales in April. Was that a special promotion? Was it one that could be repeated? Was it related to some event that might be repeated? Look at your sales data and dig in to make an educated guess about whether or not whatever happened last April will happen again next April.

I'm hoping you're noticing lots of questions. They come from the data but show up more easily when you put the data into this visual form. Consider Figure 3.2, the same basic company and lines of sales but very different past data.

I hope you see a very different picture with this visual. In this case, systems sales are falling rapidly, training is shooting up, service seems to be in a growth spurt, and software is hard to tell, it goes up and then down and back up.

The point here begins with looking at what the recent past tells you. And it's also important to understand that we're not dealing with rocket science here but just the visual representation of trends. No advance degrees required, just common sense.

Which brings me to this as a reminder: I had an early career as a market researcher. I rose to vice president level in a market research company. And I have a fancy MBA degree. But what I'm saying here is that this kind of common-sense analysis, irrespective of data analysis and expensive research, is usually the best.

You have to ask the questions though; don't just look at the chart. Ask why one sales line goes up and another down. Look for other factors,

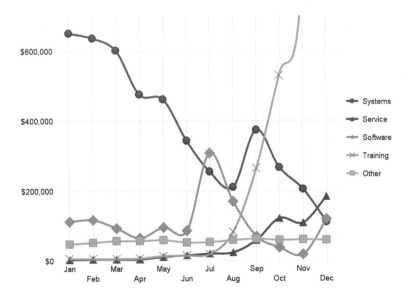

Figure 3.2. Sample line chart, alternate scenario.

like promotional spending, competitive problems, market trends, new competition, new markets. Let the numbers be the questions, and you provide the answers.

That is, at least, when you have past data to look at. This doesn't solve the problems of forecasting the new product.

Kick Tires. Look for Clues.

To me this is another common mistake with forecasting. While we're looking for sophisticated math, we forget the more obvious clues right in front of us. For example (and these are just examples; we're dealing with infinity here)

- A business has so many hours open. For some, there might be a way to project business per customer per hour. Maybe even break it into busy hours, medium hours, and slow hours (and then consider staffing during the slow hours).
- New business? Can you park across the street from an existing business of the same type? Count customers going in, and customers coming out with boxes.
- A restaurant has so many tables and chairs. It serves so many meals during lunch time and dinner, depending on hours. You can break this into examples. It cannot exceed capacity during the fullest hours. That puts a limit on things.
- A limousine service has so many cars. It can't sell more than that, even on prom night.
- Accountants and attorneys have a limited number of hours.
- Lots of businesses have upper constraints on time and people. How many hours, how many days, can they sell? Can a professional bill more hours than spent? Should they?

Research Paradox: Do It, But Don't Believe It

To my mind, the research paradox is this: Research is good but only if you don't believe it too much. How can that be?

First, Because Bad Surveys Are Rampant

I saw lots of this during the years I was a full-time professional market researcher. For example, a lot of the computer-oriented magazines would give away free subscriptions to computer industry managers but only if they filled in a questionnaire sharing how big their budget and how much computer equipment they "intended to buy" over the next few months. So I ask you: What do you think? How valuable is a survey practically asking people to exaggerate plans to purchase? And is there any reason not to exaggerate?

In addition to this example of surveys skewed toward a wrong answer, there are many surveys sent to skewed groups of target audiences, or with leading (purposely or not) questions.

And what happens, way too often, is that conclusions that would be obviously debatable in other circumstances are no longer debatable when the research supports them. They are a given. Managers don't want to go against "the research." Too bad.

Author Note: I was one of the judges at a business plan contest for the University of Notre Dame. The team was pitching a fish taco restaurant in Baton Rouge, LA. Another judge who'd had ample restaurant experience asked the team: "What makes you think they like fish tacos in Baton Rouge?"

The entrepreneurs were sure that they'd like them in Baton Rouge, essentially because they like them in San Diego.

The judge answered: "Here's what you do: Get a few trays of those fish tacos and go to the main plaza in Baton Rouge and give them all away. And then check the garbage cans on either side."

Second, Focus Groups Are Suspect

I've seen focus groups in action. They are notoriously hard to manage. The members have to be very carefully selected, which is hard, these days, because some people love going to focus groups and look for focus group opportunities. One charismatic person can change the entire results of a focus group.

Third, Settings and Definitions Mean Everything

Many years ago when I was a professional market researcher I watched a mentor, one of the smartest and most seasoned professionals I knew, handle a difficult problem with a client presentation.

The problem was that the client, one of the largest companies in the world, didn't believe our numbers. And they obviously knew way more about that particular industry than we did. The job was turning into a disaster as we delivered.

My friend and mentor, however, didn't even blink. He asked the group of client executives about their definition of this particular product group. He listened to their answer, and invented a revised definition of what we had studied, which made the numbers come back down to what our clients could believe.

I'm not recommending this kind of tactic; but I am sharing it because it happens all the time.

Research depends so much on getting the right target people, the right questions, and all the details right, that it works best with a healthy attitude of skepticism.

And I am not suggesting research is bad; what is bad is giving too much credence to research. If the discussion stays open, research is subject to question and analysis, then it becomes very valuable.

One of the best forecasting projects I've ever been involved with happened when we at Palo Alto Software were looking at developing a new line of related software products for a new target market, more expensive, more feature-rich than what we were then selling. We hired one smart woman to find ten people who were representative of the target market we were looking at, and talk to each one of them at length and in depth. When she was finished, she said our project was not going to sell well. None of the carefully selected target users wanted it.

It was more subjective than most research but much easier to believe. Our researcher had nothing to gain by positive or negative results. She was smart, and she knew how to listen. And her ten people had no preconceived notions or interest in the project.

The Web: Mountains of Needles

Ah yes, there's the rub. One of the big dampeners of sales forecasting is the impression that there's information available somewhere that provides the real answer, or the right answer. I used to believe that myself. It took several years in market research and a lot more running a company, for me to recognize that forecasting is about smart guessing, not great research.

The future, unfortunately, is not available for you at the end of a smart Web search. You're still stuck with guessing.

Having said that, however, I also want to remind myself and you that the ideal is educated guessing, not just wild guessing. And to educate those guesses, there are some kinds of information you can sometimes use.

Research for New Products and Services

And also very important, before we leave my cynical introduction to this topic, we can't forget that the problem of an initial sales forecast for a new business, new product, or new service. You don't have past data to deal

By Arthur Domagala via Shutterstock

with. You have to come up with more information to set the parameters of your guessing. And that's where research is necessary.

A good forecast begins with good information. Before you can rush to the spreadsheet analysis and technical forecasting tools, start with the right information. A standard market forecast begins with good data on basic demographics of the population, economic trends, consumption patterns, and so forth. It requires a good understanding of the products to be forecast, their use, present installations, substitute products, price trends, buying patterns, and distribution channels, among other factors. A sales forecast considers not just the whole market for a product but also competitive trends and past sales data, changing product features, new distribution channels, and other factors.

The earlier market forecasts for personal computers are a good example of the nature of professional forecasting. When personal computers first appeared, professional market forecasters had to predict a market for a product that had for all practical purposes never existed. They looked at the total population, and began to divide it by economic segments, occupations, age, gender, education, and geographic location. All of the early personal computer market forecasts assumed that the new product had a total market potential of some percentage of total households and total businesses in the United States. They differed on the percentage. They all depended on good basic information about numbers of office workers, businesses, and households.

Your own company's sales forecasts may be another example. Almost all sales forecasts start with past sales data. Future sales are projected as an extension of past and present sales. There is no better check against error than comparing a forecast to recent results.

Gathering Information

Start where you are, in your own company. Don't research the rest of the world until you have a good grasp on your own sales, broken down by product, territory, market segment, distribution channel, salesperson, or as many different ways as your company keeps information.

The Web Search

Of course the Web search is indispensable. You start with Google, Yahoo!, Bing, and their competitors. While we used to talk about information available for free in business publications, the trade press, and library reference shelves, in the market research and forecasting business, that's pretty much become obsolete.

Web searching changes. The basic skill is about choosing your search terms, using combinations of words. Different search engines have different logic, so I would not abandon a search until I looked at three different ways.

More important than how to search, and less time bound, is what to search for. What are you looking for?

And what are you looking for? You're looking for clues. Particularly when you don't have the luxury of past results, so that you can't extrapolate from the past, it's all about clues:

- Industry growth rates, trends, market behavior, and market performance, all of which matter for the trees and forest methodologies in the following two chapters.
- Basic demographics, to establish the top-end potential market and work a sales forecast based on penetration through an established group, the bell curve, idea adoption, as in chapter 6.

Industry-Specific Sites, Blogs, and Trade Press

It used to be the trade press, basically magazines focusing on certain industries. Nowadays it's Web sites and blogs focusing on certain industries. Each industry has its favorite magazine or Web site or association, from architects to zookeepers. Somebody has thought up a Web site or blog or magazine to advertise whatever that industry buys, and somebody has to write the editorial material necessary to fill the space between the ads. Often that includes regular statistics published by market research firms or industry organizations and articles that include tables, graphs, and even more statistics.

Industry-Related Information From General Business Information Sites

General business Web sites, blogs, and publications are also valuable. Journalists regularly poll industry experts for background on business news. That means you can sometimes find several expert opinions in a single story.

This kind of information is relatively easy to find. There's not just the publications' own sites (*Wall Street Journal, New York Times, Business Week, Inc. Magazine,* all searchable online) but also the wealth of blogs that cover business information angles.

You can probably already receive the important journals from your own industry, at least for those that still have journals not superseded by the Web. In some rare cases, you can also check your corporate or local library for any of several indices of business publications that list stories by industry, company, region, and so on. These have become steadily less important compared to Web search but some are still there.

Even competitive information is often available. Publicly traded companies have to publish detailed financial reports. In many industries, growth rates of industry leaders indicate growth of the industry as a whole. For example, if you have good data on the performance of Ford, Chrysler, and General Motors, then you know a lot about the U.S. domestic auto industry. Add auto imports, and you know about the auto market. Read the annual reports of industry leaders, reports published by stock analysts, brokerage houses, and business publications. All of this is going to be available on the Web.

Quality vs. Quantity Information

When in doubt, go for quality of information over quantity. Important facts and insight lot of data just because it's a lot of data.

Advice: Quality of information counts much more than the quality of numerical analysis. And quantity of numerical analysis is least important.

CHAPTER 4

Trees From the Forest

Especially when you're forecasting something new, for which you have no history, you're much more likely to have your information run from the top, the big picture, down into the details. It is then easier to take the whole market first, then divide it into smaller, more manageable pieces. This is the opposite of the ground-up (also called bottom up or forest from the trees) approach in chapter 5. I call it the "trees from the forest" method.

Kostyantin Ivanyshen via Shutterstock

The Market Share Model

Assume you are selling a new add-on gizmo that goes with a Wanderer (I made up the name) fuel-efficient sedan. You'd like to look at sales of this product over time, but of course you can't just ask your salespeople as we did in the previous chapter, because this is a brand new market and a brand new product. So you build a market share model instead.

Step one is to find or make a good, reliable whole-market forecast. If you find one instead of make one, it requires good information, as suggested in chapter 3. Most industries have forecasters at work somewhere in the background, either on a blog, or in a market research firm, a stock brokerage, or an industry association. If you had a corporate budget or a corporate planning position, then you would probably already have been working with one forecast or another. If you're a typical entrepreneur manager, then at least you know which Web sites to frequent, and whom to ask. Look for references in the blogs, the industry-specific Web sites, and references in the online business press.

Figure 4.1 has an example of a hypothetical forecast for a new product. For row 2 of the sample forecast in Figure 4.1 (*Gizmos on Wanderer (thousands)*), we used a hypothetical forecast done by a hypothetical market research house, one of several dedicated to high-tech industry forecasts. If you want to be very much up to date, you can assume we found it on the Web, after polling friends on Twitter. These forecasts appear on the Web from time to time, and if you watch your industry, be sure to bookmark them. Remember the crossword puzzle discussion, included in chapter 3.

The rest of our market share forecast depends on that initial forecast in row 2. It estimates the market for gizmos on the Wanderer as 350,000 units in 2010, growing at 66% per year through 2014. The manufacturer will be selling about 75% of the total gizmos for that model, according to our information research. However, the manufacturer's share is expected to decline steadily, to only 45% of the market in 2014. The independent suppliers will therefore pick up a growing share of the market, which makes the total market more interesting to a potential independent vendor.

Notice, as we explore this example, how much it depends on the quality of the information in row 2. If this source of the market forecast is wrong, the rest of the forecast will be wrong too. Every line of the model depends on the accuracy of the industry forecast in row 2. This is all hypothetical in this case, but real forecasts often depend on industry data in the same way this sample one does.

There is also a silver lining to this dependence. If you can put a name onto the source forecast—the Web site, the market research firm, the industry expert—then your initial product forecast is validated, in the eyes

◇	A	B	C	D	E	F	G
		2010	2011	2012	2013	2014	Average
1	Sales Projection						
2	Gizmos on Wanderer (thousands)	350	700	1,248	1,956	2,640	66%
3	Growth %	n.a.	100%	78%	57%	35%	
4	Manufacturer share %	75%	66%	58%	51%	45%	-12%
5	Manufacturer share thousands	263	462	724	998	1,188	46%
6	Independents share %	25%	34%	42%	49%	55%	22%
7	Independents share (thousands)	88	238	524	958	1,452	102%
8	Our company share %	25%	35%	45%	55%	65%	27%
9	Our company share (thousands)	22	83	236	527	944	156%
10	Manufacturer average price	$179.00	$179.00	$179.00	$179.00	$179.00	0%
11	Independent average price	$129.00	$114.00	$100.00	$80.00	$65.00	-16%
12	Our average price	$99.00	$99.00	$79.00	$69.00	$59.00	-12%
13	Our sales (thousands)	$2,166	$8,247	$18,634	$36,373	$55,684	125%

Figure 4.1. Market share model.

of most observers, by the use of the generally accepted source. It gives a forecast more weight as validating the possibilities for a new product.

Spreadsheet Details

This example makes use of several common spreadsheet tips. I'll point some of them out here in detail. Most of them are a matter of making your life simpler.

The Dateline Row

The dateline row sets a starting date, the year 2010, in cell B1. The formula for cell C1, which has 2011 in it, is

$$= B1 + 1.$$

With that formula set for C1, you can select the cells C1:F1 and use the *Copy Right* facility of the spreadsheet to make the dateline row automatically, without having to type each year. In Microsoft Excel, that *Copy Right* can be executed with a *Ctrl-R* key.

This is a very simple example, but it does give a good view of making spreadsheets easier to manage for the long term. To change the starting year in this forecast, say a year from now, you would only need to change the first year. The next changes automatically. There's more on this in chapter 10.

Compound Average Growth Rate Formula

Compound average growth rate (CAGR) calculations are quite useful. Whenever you shave sales or markets increasing over time, you can produce an average growth rate for a period by knowing the starting value, the ending value, and the amount of time. In row 2 of Figure 4.1, for example, growth from 350,000 in 2010 to 2.6 million in 2014 is an average growth rate of 66% per year. Figure 4.2 shows that formula in an Excel formula edit bar so you can see it.

The CAGR formula is used in column G, in rows 2, 4, 5, 6, 8, 9, 11, 12, and 13. It uses an important standard financial analysis formula.

G2	▾	f_x =(F2/B2)^(1/4)-1					
	f_x	=(F2/B2)^(1/4)-1	B	C	D	E	F	G
1	Sales Projection		2010	2011	2012	2013	2014 Average
2	Gizmos on Wanderer (thousands)		350	700	1,248	1,956	2,640	66%

Figure 4.2. CAGR formula illustrated.

Given the starting point, the end point, and the number of growth periods, it calculates an average growth rate over that specified time. The basic formula is

CAGR = (ending value/Starting value) ^ (1/periods) – 1.

That same formula is used here in cell G2, which computes the average growth rate of the whole market, from 2010 to 2014:

= (F2/B2)^(1/4) – 1.

In this case, F2 is the final value (2.640 million) and B2 is the starting value (350,000). The number of periods is four, not five, because there are only 4 years of growth: 2011, 2012, 2013, and 2014. The first year of the forecast, 2010, does not have a growth rate because we are ignoring 2009.

The caret (^) refers to exponents. I'm sorry, this is real math. For example 2^3 is spoken as "two raised to the third power," or 2*2*2, which is 8. Where we see this most often is with the second power, which is referred to as squared. So

3^2

would mean three squared, which is equal to 9, the product of multiplying three by three. The third power, as in 2^3, is also called cubed. So

3^3

would be 3*3*3, or three times three times three, which is 27. In the CAGR formula, the result of ending/starting is raised to the 1/periods power. Then the number one is subtracted from the result.

You can see in Figure 4.1 how the CAGR formula works for different rows. There's more on the formulas and math of CAGR in chapter 10.

Model Logic and Structure

The market share model in Figure 4.1 takes the information in its rows 2 and 3 from some reliable forecast. Then we derive resulting market values and our own shares in the rest of the model. In row 4, we build an assumption about the share of total that will be won by the manufacturer. This important assumption is based on good research, experts guessing, on the Web, or not. It may be derived from published forecasts, or good forecasting. It is a good example of a professional educated guess.

The CAGR figure in cell G4 refers to the average decline in manufacturer's share as it drops from 75% to 45%. This is another educated guess, looking at trends. Then in row 5 we calculate the units value of the manufacturer's share by multiplying the whole market by the percentage assigned to the manufacturer. This is a simple formula. The CAGR calculation in cell G5 tells us the average growth of the manufacturer's unit sales.

The key here is tying assumptions together, logically, so that one flows to another and the end result is believable. To make a good forecast, you have to pore over those assumptions, change them, reevaluate them, and finally decide you can live with them—which, by the way, is also called *scenario analysis*.

Row 6 is another simple calculation. The independent's market share is a direct function of the main manufacturer's market share. So the formula in row 6 subtracts row 4 from 1. And row 7, just like row 5, is simple multiplication of the whole market by the percentage assumed for the independents.

Row 8 contains the most important assumption in the model and also the one with the highest degree of uncertainty. Here we guess what our company's share of the independents' units will be. This once again has to be an educated guess, based on what research is available, comparison of products, distribution channels, buyer patterns, advertising and promotion, and whatever other factors we can think of. In our example, we are saying that our company is going to be able to increase its share substantially during the forecast period. Why? How much is that going to cost?

What will competition do about it? Will technology change too quickly? There are many questions implied in that row of assumptions. And one of the answers is placed very clearly in the play between rows 10 and 12, in which we see the assumed price differential between manufacturer's product, the independents' products, and our specific product.

Row 9 is the calculated result of the previous assumptions. One of the things I really like about spreadsheets and spreadsheet logic is the way you can follow the assumptions down the path to the conclusions, visually, within the spreadsheet model. Once we accept the whole market forecast, the share breakdowns, and our own share in the independents, then we have to accept row 9, which is simple mathematics. If we don't, then we have to go back and adjust our assumptions.

Row 13, my personal favorite, is the sales revenue conclusion to the forecast. This one looks like the kind of high growth projection that backs a venture looking for professional investment. And notice how it works for confidence and validation. Put yourself in the place of somebody projecting sales of a product to hit $2 million in your company's launch year and grow to more than $50 million 5 years later. Figure 4.3 shows you the slide you might present to investors.

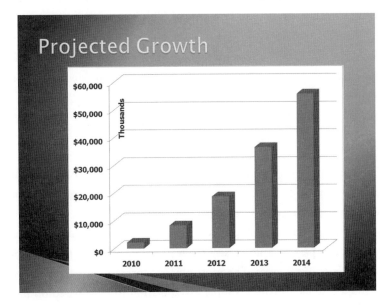

Figure 4.3. Sales projection slide.

Consider how much better you feel, and the investors as well, when you can justify the sales forecast in this presentation based on step-by-step assumptions in the model. It's still a fabulous growth rate, perhaps still way higher than what is credible; but the assumptions make it much easier to defend.

Always Question Assumptions

This is also a good example of why you should approach these models with some skepticism. Always question the assumptions, use the worksheet to run the model with different sets of assumptions, and watch how quickly the results change. Figure 4.4 shows how quickly results can change when assumptions change.

In this second case, the model is almost the same, but two assumptions have changed. In row 4, we assume the manufacturer holds share better than in the previous run. In row 8, we assume our company fails to build its share as planned, with the independents' share lower. And you can see in rows 10–12 how we've assumed different pricing behavior as well; that partially explains the other assumptions.

The chart in Figure 4.5 demonstrates the difference, the shortfall between the first scenario and the second. This is not a pretty picture.

The market share model like this one can be very useful. As with the rest of this book, please remember that this is just one example of infinite variations. Use this example to think about how this kind of forecast might work for your business, in your specific situation.

Chain Method Forecast

The chain method is a useful variation of the market share method. In this case, you have a series of related facts, from which you can draw an ever-sharper picture of your targeted piece of information.

The sample model here projects the sales at popcorn concessions at a movie complex in a university town of about 150,000 people. The forecast goes out 3 years. The most obvious forecast, and certainly the best in a case like this, is a simple extrapolation forecast based on past sales. In this example, however, we assume a hypothetical but quite

	A	B	C	D	E	F	G
		2010	2011	2012	2013	2014	Average
1	Sales Projection						
2	Gizmos on Wanderer (thousands)	350	700	1,248	1,956	2,640	66%
3	Growth %	n.a.	100%	78%	57%	35%	
4	Manufacturer share %	75%	74%	72%	71%	70%	-2%
5	Manufacturer share thousands	263	518	899	1,389	1,848	63%
6	Independents share %	25%	26%	28%	29%	30%	5%
7	Independents share (thousands)	88	182	349	567	792	73%
8	Our company share %	25%	26%	28%	29%	30%	5%
9	Our company share (thousands)	22	47	98	164	238	82%
10	Manufacturer average price	$179.00	$140.00	$110.00	$90.00	$70.00	-21%
11	Independent average price	$129.00	$100.00	$80.00	$60.00	$50.00	-21%
12	Our average price	$99.00	$80.00	$60.00	$50.00	$40.00	-20%
13	Our sales (thousands)	$2,166	$3,786	$5,871	$8,225	$9,504	45%

Figure 4.4. Changed assumptions.

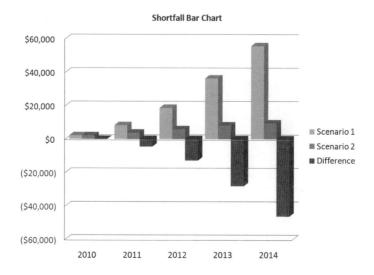

Figure 4.5. Shortfall bar chart.

common business situation for the entrepreneur. We're buying the theater, or projecting concession revenues, but we can't use past data because the former operator kept very poor records. Also, we want to produce some objective measure of reasonable sales expectations on our own, rather than use someone else's numbers: the people selling the concessions may have ulterior motives in overestimating the sales. So we built the chain forecast shown in Figure 4.6.

	A	B	C	D	E
1		Assumption	2010	2011	2012
2	Households	2%	53,000	54,060	55,141
3	Average household income	2%	$57,500	$58,650	$59,823
4	Entertainment (millions)	5.4%	$165	$171	$178
5	Cinema (millions)	3%	$4.9	$5.1	$5.3
6	Popcorn (thousands)	10%	$494	$514	$534
7	Market share		20%	22%	24%
8	Sales Forecast		$99	$113	$128

Figure 4.6. Chain method.

Design for Assumptions Analysis

The model assumptions are built in. In row 2, for example, the 2% growth assumption in cell B2 drives the population assumptions in cells D2 and E2. The formula for D2 is

$$= C2*(1 + \$B2).$$

In row 3, the $57,500 average household income assumption determines the values for cells C3 through E3. In row 4, we assume 5.4% of household income is spent on entertainment (which comes from visualeconomics.com, by the way, which cites the U.S. Department of Labor as a source for consumer spending). In row 5, we assume 3% of that is spent on cinema; and in row 6, 10% of that on popcorn. Then in the final two rows, this spreadsheet looks a lot like another market share model as we assume a market share and then calculate the resulting sales forecast.

Built-in assumptions are easy to change. You can change any of the assumption rows in this model, except the final market share, by changing its assumption value in column B. This design simplifies later analysis.

In the sample model we have numbers denominated in millions, percents, and thousands. I hope you see why I don't bother pulling these estimated numbers into finer cuts, like more decimals. They are estimates and look better in larger summarized numbers, which makes it clearer that they are estimates. I did use simple spreadsheet formatting commands to improve the visual effect, and I varied the zeros as required to not have very large numbers. The formula for cell C4, for example, is

$$= (\$B4*C2*C3)/1000000.$$

Adjusting the denominations as shown in the chain model may be necessary at times, but it is always dangerous. It adds an important new source of potential error. Use adjustments like these only when needed and with great care. When you adjust denominations like this, remember to specify denominations in row labels.

Information Inputs

Much of the data in forecasting depends on general economic information. You might look at the economic indicators available through government Web sites including business.gov and others. You can also use Web searches to see what other statistics might be available from trade groups and other sources, plus information Web sites, publications, and trade associations. You may often have to estimate an important number—and if you do, it's far better to estimate with the chain method than by just starting from scratch with no information.

The chain forecast looks simple enough to do by hand on paper and not by computer on a spreadsheet program. Sometimes it is. But normally there are estimates that have to be polished through trial and error. And there are good reasons to look at what would happen if some of the key percentages were to change. What if disposable income drops by a percentage point or people spent 5% instead of 3% of their entertainment money on the movies. What about Netflix, or Amazon Unbox? How might they affect the outlook? Is there research available for other markets? The spreadsheet gives you a lot of power to question the model, vary the assumptions, and consider alternate scenarios.

CHAPTER 5

Forest From the Trees

For forest-from-the-trees or bottom-up forecasting, you break your problem down into smaller pieces, work on the pieces, and then add them up again to get the whole picture. This is particularly useful for forecasting sales. It is often easier to forecast each detail separately and then to add up the details to produce a complete forecast.

We're just human, so we can't see the future as accurately as we'd like. It helps, though, to break the problem into smaller parts. Look at the parts in detail, then add them back up. I think this is often the better way to do it because we can see the parts more easily than we can see the whole—the trees more than the forest.

In this chapter, we look at a forecast that starts with an easy-to-understand detail and accumulates more detail to build an entire forecast. The example we show is a customer poll forecast: Each customer's own projections of next year's sales are combined to make an entire sales forecast.

By Timothy Epp via Shutterstock

There are many other ways to produce a bottom-up forecast. Perhaps you're working on a restaurant and you project tables and seats per table and then hours open and meals per table at various hours. Or you're working on a Web site and you project unique visits, purchases per visitor; or you're paying pay-per-click ads on the Web and you project conversions per click. In all these cases, you work the detail first, then the whole.

One of the easiest sales forecasts to make is based on an actual poll of customers. This is sometimes possible in an industrial context, in which sales are composed of large volumes of material or high-priced items sold to only a few very important customers.

In this case you ask your customers what they'll need next year, then add it all up. The spreadsheet details are quite simple: Label your rows for customers, label your columns for months and years, fill in the blanks and then add them up. Smith's Worksheet in Figure 5.1 is an example. Salesman Smith asked her customers what they plan to order for 2011. She added the numbers up and produced a forecast.

Not bad for a start, but that's certainly simple enough to do on a piece of paper with a pencil, rather than on a computer spreadsheet.

Author Note: Notice the check line in cell F7. I learned the hard way to build check lines into spreadsheet forecasts whenever possible. Mistakes are hard to see when the output is all straight and looks printed and organized. So check when you can. More on that in chapter 10.

Asking the Customers

Now suppose we have several regions to deal with and several salespersons in each region, each salesperson dealing with several companies. Some of the companies have different local operations and buy from two or three of the salesmen in their local area. Then we have to build a forecast more carefully. We have a lot more incentive to use the spreadsheet.

Now we ask Salesman Jones and Saleswoman Mitchell to do the same, to produce the worksheet shown in Figure 5.2, the customer poll worksheet. It's about the same as Smith's worksheet but it also includes the two other salespeople's data.

The math and mechanics of all this are very simple.

	A	B	C	D	E	F
1		Q1-11	Q2-11	Q3-11	Q4-11	FY-2011
2	Cust A	$35	$45	$60	$40	$180
3	Cust B	$30	$30	$30	$30	$120
4	Cust C	$80	$100	$120	$110	$410
5	Others	$14	$18	$23	$19	$74
6	Total	$159	$193	$233	$199	$784
7	Check					784

Figure 5.1. Smith's worksheet.

	A	B	C	D	E	F
1	Cust	Q1-11	Q2-11	Q3-11	Q4-11	FY-2011
2	Smith					
3	Cust A	$35	$45	$60	$40	$180
4	Cust B	$30	$30	$30	$30	$120
5	Cust C	$80	$100	$120	$110	$410
6	Others	$14	$18	$23	$19	$74
7	Smith Total	$159	$193	$233	$199	$784
8	Jones					
9	Cust B	$45	$45	$45	$45	$180
10	Cust D	$55	$65	$75	$70	$265
11	Cust E	$85	$100	$120	$100	$405
12	Cust F	$20	$25	$35	$25	$105
13	Others	$13	$18	$22	$16	$69
14	Jones Total	$218	$253	$297	$256	$1,024
15	Mitchell					
16	Cust A	$50	$65	$75	$70	$260
17	Cust B	$120	$130	$140	$150	$540
18	Cust E	$42	$52	$56	$47	$197
19	Cust G	$25	$35	$45	$35	$140
20	Others	$17	$19	$23	$17	$76
21	Mitchell Total	$254	$301	$339	$319	$1,213
22	Grand Totals	$631	$747	$869	$774	$3,021
23						$3,021

Figure 5.2. Customer poll worksheet.

	A	B	C	D	E	F
24	Cust A	$85	$110	$135	$110	$440
25	Cust B	$195	$205	$215	$225	$840
26	Cust C	$80	$100	$120	$110	$410
27	Cust D	$55	$65	$75	$70	$265
28	Cust E	$127	$152	$176	$147	$602
29	Cust F	$20	$25	$35	$25	$105
30	Cust G	$25	$35	$45	$35	$140
31	Others	$44	$55	$68	$52	$219
32	Grand Totals	$631	$747	$869	$774	$3,021

Figure 5.3. Customer totals.

If you're working on a spreadsheet that you've programmed yourself, make sure to add in a check line.

The check line may be the most valuable suggestion in this book. A computer will sometimes hide "dumb" mistakes. It's easy to add the wrong two lines together; the output looks so nice that you never know it until you've already gone to the bank with it. That's embarrassing.

The check line checks your figures by adding them in a different way. By adding a check line like the one in these models, you'll catch at least some of those errors. If the "total by salesperson" doesn't check the "total by customer," then there's an error—and it isn't a computer error.

To add an error-check row to Figure 5.2, you might add all the customer totals together to see that the total, when broken down by customer, is equal to the total by salesperson.

Incorporate Graphics

Graphic representations of numbers are sometimes easier to evaluate than the numbers themselves. Often you can improve your understanding of a forecast by looking at a graphic version. We can do a sample graph with the forecast data we have in Figure 5.2.

Or it could be more useful to show the total sales in a different bar chart, as shown in Figure 5.5.

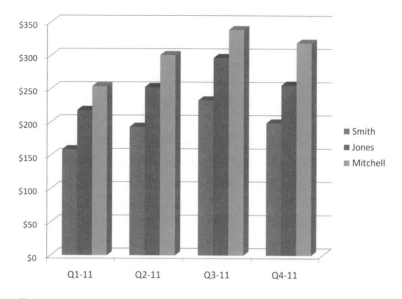

Figure 5.4. Simple bar chart.

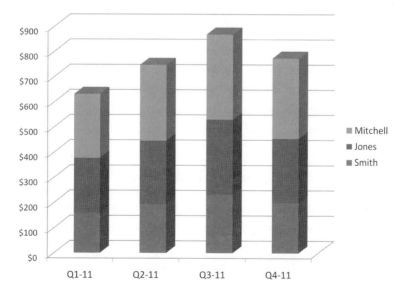

Figure 5.5. Stacked bar chart.

Asking Questions

Please remember, however, that as impressive as pretty charts are, as much as they can add to the presentation of numbers, their relevance to forecasting is much more than cosmetic. Use these graphs to evaluate the forecast. What questions does it bring to mind? Should the third quarter be higher than the fourth? Has it been in past years? Why does Smith consistently sell less than Jones or Mitchell? Has this been true in the past? Are there reasons for this trend to continue? Are the territories unequal?

Questions like these move us toward the topic of data analysis, or data massage. We use those terms with some cynicism, frankly, because we think most people overestimate the technical side of data analysis. When it comes to a real forecast of a real business, "massage" is a better word. You will rarely find fancy techniques that work better than taking a good hard look at the numbers, testing them in your own mind for reasonableness. That's why graphs are so good, because they provide instant analysis with bumps and sharp curves and trend lines. Often, the key is not asking the right question, but rather, asking enough questions.

With the sample forecast, we now have a combination that looks good on paper. We have neat tables, pretty printed copy, and even graphs…but is the forecast reasonable? (Don't ask if it's right or not: It's a forecast; by definition it's not right.) So far, we have depended completely on our customers' own forecast of their future purchases. We should question the quality of our information. Maybe the customers inflated their projections because they think that guarantees a trouble-free supply of raw materials. Are they being too optimistic or too pessimistic? We can't really rely on a forecast until we've considered these alternatives.

Looking at Past Trends

There is no better forecasting technique than comparing future forecasts to past results, understanding the trends, and projection them forward.

Of course this method, like any other, is far from foolproof. You can't simply project the future from the past. Things change, curves go up and down; you must constantly check for reasonableness, sensitive assumptions, and new factors.

Many of the more respected forecasting techniques, including regression analysis and econometric market models, are variations on projecting the past into the future. That doesn't make them right or reasonable. At the very least, however, when you project a variation from past trends you should be able to explain why.

The past data worksheet shown in Figure 5.6 takes the next logical step in the forecast process. After we poll our customers, we should go back and compare their future forecasts to their past results. We use data from 2010 to compare to our 2011 forecast.

The presentation of the numbers in Figure 5.6 simplifies comparisons from 2010 to 2011. We can look at growth rates as numbers, or better year, as a graph. The chart in Figure 5.7 shows the data in graphic form.

◇	A	B	C	D	E	F	G	H	I	J
1	Cust	Q1-10	Q2-10	Q3-10	Q4-10	Q1-11	Q2-11	Q3-11	Q4-11	FY-2011
2	Smith									
3	Cust A	$29	$36	$51	$31	$35	$45	$60	$40	$180
4	Cust B	$21	$23	$26	$24	$30	$30	$30	$30	$120
5	Cust C	$60	$64	$75	$59	$80	$100	$120	$110	$410
6	Others	$12	$15	$19	$16	$14	$18	$23	$19	$74
7	Smith Total	$122	$138	$171	$130	$159	$193	$233	$199	$784
8	Jones									
9	Cust B	$31	$35	$39	$35	$45	$45	$45	$45	$180
10	Cust D	$42	$54	$61	$53	$55	$65	$75	$70	$265
11	Cust E	$67	$81	$94	$50	$85	$100	$120	$100	$405
12	Cust F	$15	$21	$28	$19	$20	$25	$35	$25	$105
13	Others	$11	$15	$18	$13	$13	$18	$22	$16	$69
14	Jones Total	$166	$206	$240	$170	$218	$253	$297	$256	$1,024
15	Mitchell									
16	Cust A	$40	$52	$61	$55	$50	$65	$75	$70	$260
17	Cust B	$85	$105	$128	$120	$120	$130	$140	$150	$540
18	Cust E	$35	$43	$47	$39	$42	$52	$56	$47	$197
19	Cust G	$18	$25	$30	$20	$25	$35	$45	$35	$140
20	Others	$14	$16	$19	$14	$17	$19	$23	$17	$76
21	Mitchell Total	$192	$241	$285	$248	$254	$301	$339	$319	$1,213
22	Grand Totals	$480	$585	$696	$548	$631	$747	$869	$774	$3,021
23										$3,021
24	Cust A	$69	$88	$112	$86	$85	$110	$135	$110	$440
25	Cust B	$137	$163	$193	$179	$195	$205	$215	$225	$840
26	Cust C	$60	$64	$75	$59	$80	$100	$120	$110	$410
27	Cust D	$42	$54	$61	$53	$55	$65	$75	$70	$265
28	Cust E	$102	$124	$141	$89	$127	$152	$176	$147	$602
29	Cust F	$15	$21	$28	$19	$20	$25	$35	$25	$105
30	Cust G	$18	$25	$30	$20	$25	$35	$45	$35	$140
31	Others	$37	$46	$56	$43	$44	$55	$68	$52	$219
32	Grand Totals	$480	$585	$696	$548	$631	$747	$869	$774	$3,021

Figure 5.6. Looking at the recent past.

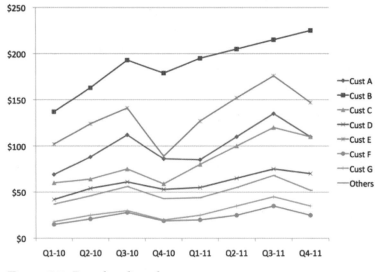

Figure 5.7. Past data line chart.

Graphic View

Most people visualize better with the graph. Follow the lines of the different customers as they move from each of the four quarters of 2010—which is real, actual sales in the recent past—to their projections for each of the quarters of 2011. There are some danger signs. Business generally drops in the fourth quarter, but customer B and to some extent customer D ignore that trend. Customer E is projecting very strong growth in 2011, and a sharp drop at the end. This seems to fit with their results in 2010.

Looking at Growth Rates

Don't depend completely on the graphs. The numbers involved are also important. The worksheet in Figure 5.8 shows the growth rates from each quarter to the same quarter of the previous year. Some of the numbers in the worksheet are highlighted, because they should stand out to the forecaster. Graphs help and so do the numbers.

The worksheet in Figure 5.8 is a simple, but extremely practical, spreadsheet data analysis. The percentage growth formulas are based on a simple standard formula:

$$\%Growth = (this\ year/last\ year) - 1.$$

This formula runs across most of the cells in the worksheet. It picks up the actual year-by-year data from the previous worksheet in Figure 5.6, using linked worksheets.

The worksheet highlights (using format commands) some particularly interesting rows. The average growth for the forecast is about 30%—that is in cell G24 and also in the check line cell, G28. However, some of the customers are projecting growth well above the standard 30% level.

◇	A	B	C	D	E	F	G
1	Cust		Q1-11	Q2-11	Q3-11	Q4-11	FY-2011
2	Cust A	Smith	20.7%	25.0%	17.6%	29.0%	22.4%
3	Cust B	Smith	42.9%	30.4%	15.4%	25.0%	27.7%
4	**Cust C**	**Smith**	**33.3%**	**56.3%**	**60.0%**	**86.4%**	**58.9%**
5	Others	Smith	16.7%	20.0%	21.1%	18.8%	19.4%
6	Cust B	Jones	45.2%	28.6%	15.4%	28.6%	28.6%
7	Cust D	Jones	31.0%	20.4%	23.0%	32.1%	26.2%
8	Cust E	Jones	26.9%	23.5%	27.7%	100.0%	38.7%
9	Cust F	Jones	33.3%	19.0%	25.0%	31.6%	26.5%
10	Others	Jones	18.2%	20.0%	22.2%	23.1%	21.1%
11	Cust A	Mitchell	25.0%	25.0%	23.0%	27.3%	25.0%
12	Cust B	Mitchell	41.2%	23.8%	9.4%	25.0%	23.3%
13	Cust E	Mitchell	20.0%	20.9%	19.1%	20.5%	20.1%
14	**Cust G**	**Mitchell**	**38.9%**	**40.0%**	**50.0%**	**75.0%**	**50.5%**
15	Others	Mitchell	21.4%	18.8%	21.1%	21.4%	20.6%
16	Cust A	Total	23.2%	25.0%	20.5%	27.9%	23.9%
17	Cust B	Total	42.3%	25.8%	11.4%	25.7%	25.0%
18	**Cust C**	**Total**	**33.3%**	**56.3%**	**60.0%**	**86.4%**	**58.9%**
19	Cust D	Total	31.0%	20.4%	23.0%	32.1%	26.2%
20	Cust E	Total	24.5%	22.6%	24.8%	65.2%	32.0%
21	Cust F	Total	33.3%	19.0%	25.0%	31.6%	26.5%
22	**Cust G**	**Total**	**38.9%**	**40.0%**	**50.0%**	**75.0%**	**50.5%**
23	Others	Total	18.9%	19.6%	21.4%	20.9%	20.3%
24	**Grand Totals**		31.5%	27.7%	24.9%	41.2%	30.8%
25	Total	Smith	30.3%	39.9%	36.3%	53.1%	39.8%
26	Total	Jones	31.3%	22.8%	23.8%	50.6%	30.9%
27	Total	Mitchell	32.3%	24.9%	18.9%	28.6%	25.6%
28	**Check Total**		31.5%	27.7%	24.9%	41.2%	30.8%

Figure 5.8. Past growth numbers.

Notice in Figure 5.8 that customer C is planning to increase almost 60% and customer G more than 50%.

These high forecasts from particular customers bring us back to the basics of forecasting. We need quality information. At this point, the forecaster should go back to salespeople Mitchell and Smith for more information about the customers' projected growth. We might want to talk to the customers themselves. Why are they intending to increase? New customers? New plant? New related product, more salespeople, lower prices, or some other reason? Judgment is required. Should the forecast take the customers at their word, or second guess them? In a real forecast situation, these questions would have to be answered.

We also want to highlight trends. Notice that the business almost always goes up in the second and third quarter and then down in the fourth quarter. In this case, although the spreadsheet doesn't show it here, we can use the same techniques to calculate growth in previous years. Assume the business grows about 20% in 2010 and each quarter grew about 20% over the previous year. Is the 30% growth for 2011 reasonable? It may be that because of changes in the market, increased growth is possible. Do we know that? Can we check it?

Reality Check: Data Massage and Analysis

When you're working with real data you will want to go over it in 50 different ways. Look at the percentage growth by customer. Take the percent from 2010 to 2011. Watch whether the small companies grew at the same rate as the large companies. Look at whether one or two important customers are responsible for all the growth, or are lagging. Whose production is increasing, and whose is falling off? You want to get a good solid feel for what is going on in this business.

Now it's time to look at some alternative forecasts and to compare them with our customer-driven forecast. We may decide to keep the customer-driven one, but we'll feel better about it after having compared it with some others.

In Figure 5.9 we assumed every customer is going to increase orders by exactly 10% in each quarter over the same quarter of the previous year.

We do this by building a percentage growth rate box in our model. It makes the growth rate a variable we can change at will, without changing a lot of different cell formulas. This is always a good way to treat variables in your models.

In the worksheet in Figure 5.9, the growth rates are in row 34. The cells that refer to the 2011 forecast data, in the block G2:J15, are modified to pick up the growth rate assumption in row 34. The best way to do it is by naming the cells F34:I34 *Growth rate*. For that, you'll want to look at your spreadsheet manual for how to name certain ranges; it's different for various versions of the spreadsheet.

◇	A	C	D	E	F	G	H	I	J
1	Cust	Q2-10	Q3-10	Q4-10	Q1-11	Q2-11	Q3-11	Q4-11	FY-2011
2	Smith								
3	Cust A	$36	$51	$31	$32	$40	$56	$34	$162
4	Cust B	$23	$26	$24	$23	$25	$29	$26	$103
5	Cust C	$64	$75	$59	$66	$70	$83	$65	$284
6	Others	$15	$19	$16	$13	$17	$21	$18	$68
7	Smith Total	$138	$171	$130	$134	$152	$188	$143	$617
8	Jones								
9	Cust B	$35	$39	$35	$34	$39	$43	$39	$154
10	Cust D	$54	$61	$53	$46	$59	$67	$58	$231
11	Cust E	$81	$94	$50	$74	$89	$103	$55	$321
12	Cust F	$21	$28	$19	$17	$23	$31	$21	$91
13	Others	$15	$18	$13	$12	$17	$20	$14	$63
14	Jones Total	$206	$240	$170	$183	$227	$264	$187	$860
15	Mitchell								
16	Cust A	$52	$61	$55	$44	$57	$67	$61	$229
17	Cust B	$105	$128	$120	$94	$116	$141	$132	$482
18	Cust E	$43	$47	$39	$39	$47	$52	$43	$180
19	Cust G	$25	$30	$20	$20	$28	$33	$22	$102
20	Others	$16	$19	$14	$15	$18	$21	$15	$69
21	Mitchell Total	$241	$285	$248	$211	$265	$314	$273	$1,063
22	Grand Totals	$585	$696	$548	$528	$644	$766	$603	$2,540
23									
24	Cust A	$88	$112	$86	$76	$97	$123	$95	$391
25	Cust B	$163	$193	$179	$151	$179	$212	$197	$739
26	Cust C	$64	$75	$59	$66	$70	$83	$65	$284
27	Cust D	$54	$61	$53	$46	$59	$67	$58	$231
28	Cust E	$124	$141	$89	$112	$136	$155	$98	$502
29	Cust F	$21	$28	$19	$17	$23	$31	$21	$91
30	Cust G	$25	$30	$20	$20	$28	$33	$22	$102
31	Others	$46	$56	$43	$41	$51	$62	$47	$200
32	Grand Totals	$585	$696	$548	$528	$644	$766	$603	$2,540
33									
34	Growth rate:				10%	10%	10%	10%	

Figure 5.9. The 10% growth scenario.

The beauty of doing it this way is that now we can change our growth rates easily and quickly. We can do that for each quarter if we want, although the example sticks with 10% growth throughout. By changing the growth rate constant and then recalculating the matrix, we'll get a new percentage growth rate applied to the entire worksheet.

We didn't like the 10% growth rate. When we compared it to the customer-driven forecast, it is way off. The customers are projecting more than 3,000 units and the 10% forecast means barely 2,500 units. Furthermore, sales grew at about 20% in 2010, as we know from the previous analysis, so why not 20% again?

We used the same model to produce a 20% assumption, which is shown (totals only) in Figure 5.10. Since we wrote the constant percentage growth rate into the model, we can go from the one assumption to the other very quickly. But even at 20% growth, we still have fewer units than in our customer forecast, and still by a fairly large margin.

This is where we add human common sense to the computer analysis. Go out and look at the market you're talking about. Call some customers, talk to the editors of some trade magazines, read the blogs, do the right Web searches. Is the industry going to grow 20% again? If not, then how much more or less? Our customer-driven forecast total of 3,020 is fully 31% more than our 2010 sales. What seems to be going on in the industry? Is a 31% growth rate for 2011 realistic?

◇	A	C	D	E	F	G	H	I	J
1	Cust	Q2-10	Q3-10	Q4-10	Q1-11	Q2-11	Q3-11	Q4-11	FY-2011
23									
24	Cust A	$88	$112	$86	$83	$106	$134	$103	$426
25	Cust B	$163	$193	$179	$164	$196	$232	$215	$806
26	Cust C	$64	$75	$59	$72	$77	$90	$71	$310
27	Cust D	$54	$61	$53	$50	$65	$73	$64	$252
28	Cust E	$124	$141	$89	$122	$149	$169	$107	$547
29	Cust F	$21	$28	$19	$18	$25	$34	$23	$100
30	Cust G	$25	$30	$20	$22	$30	$36	$24	$112
31	Others	$46	$56	$43	$44	$55	$67	$52	$218
32	Grand Totals	$585	$696	$548	$576	$702	$835	$658	$2,771
33									
34	Growth rate:				20%	20%	20%	20%	

Figure 5.10. 20% growth rate assumption.

Notice that we are in a trial and error process. If you like computer buzzwords, you can call that an *iterative* process. We go back and forth with the spreadsheet until we like what we have: call that *interactive iteration*.

After a period of study, we come back with the conclusion that the industry isn't growing 30% in 2011. It should rack up another 20% increase (not bad) but the rest is due to overoptimism, or the buyers' natural inclination to overestimate their purchases, or both factors at once. So now what do we do?

What we do now is guess again. But this time we incorporate the information we have from different sources. Certainly our customers have a lot to add to our forecast. But let's use the 20% number to temper their guesses. Now the spreadsheet comes into play again.

Figure 5.11 provides a way to look at the difference between 20% growth and the customer forecast. It was done with Excel's Paste Special command, which allows us to subtract (or add, multiply, or divide) one entire block from another. Other spreadsheets have similar capabilities.

This model shows the difference between the customer forecast and the 20% growth forecast. In each entry, we see how far the customer forecast falls above or below the 20% forecast. A positive number means that much more than 20% growth, and a negative number means that much less, and a blank means exactly 20% growth.

Once we have that worksheet on the computer screen, we begin to see what might be pushing the forecast up. Customer C in salesman Smith's zone is projecting a huge increase in that plant. Customer B seems to be trying to smooth out production schedules by doing more in the first quarter and less in the third quarter and is also projecting a large increase in overall purchases. Customer E looks like the buyer forgot to project the standard 15%–25% decrease in purchases in the fourth quarter. Customer G's increase is fairly large for a small plant.

So we get back on the phone. Call customers B, C, and E, and ask them about their projected orders increase. Customer C, it turns out, has a new plant production increase coming on stream and will need more units. But when asked to think about it, Customer C's buyer agrees that the start-up will be slower than that and will therefore require fewer units.

◇	A	F	G	H	I	J	K
1	Cust		Q1-11	Q2-11	Q3-11	Q4-11	FY-2011
2	Smith						
3	Cust A	Smith	$0	$2	($1)	$3	$4
4	Cust B	Smith	$5	$2	($1)	$1	$7
5	Cust C	Smith	$8	$23	$30	$39	$100
6	Others	Smith	($0)	$0	$0	($0)	($0)
9	Cust B	Jones	$8	$3	($2)	$3	$12
10	Cust D	Jones	$5	$0	$2	$6	$13
11	Cust E	Jones	$5	$3	$7	$40	$55
12	Cust F	Jones	$2	($0)	$1	$2	$5
13	Others	Jones	($0)	$0	$0	$0	$1
16	Cust A	Mitchell	$2	$3	$2	$4	$10
17	Cust B	Mitchell	$18	$4	($14)	$6	$14
18	Cust E	Mitchell	$0	$0	($0)	$0	$0
19	Cust G	Mitchell	$3	$5	$9	$11	$28
20	Others	Mitchell	$0	($0)	$0	$0	$0
21	Mitchell Total		$24	$12	($3)	$21	$54
22	Grand Totals		$55	$45	$34	$116	$250
23							
24	Cust A		$2.2	$4	$1	$7	$14
25	Cust B		$31	$9	($17)	$10	$34
26	Cust C		$8	$23	$30	$39	$100
27	Cust D		$5	$0	$2	$6	$13
28	Cust E		$5	$3	$7	$40	$55
29	Cust F		$2	($0)	$1	$2	$5
30	Cust G		$3	$5	$9	$11	$28
31	Others		($0)	($0)	$1	$0	$1
32	Grand Totals		$55	$45	$34	$116	$250

Figure 5.11. Comparison vs. 20% growth.

A Final Forecast

Then we go back to those differences and modify them to reflect what the buyers told us. The final customer poll forecast in Figure 5.12 shows how we decided to change the excesses. Compare it to the 10% growth scenario. We allowed some of the increases for most of the customers planning an increase. We also figured that we'll deliver as much as they want in the first quarter but that some of those who receive a lot of units in the first quarter will want less than they think in the second, third, and fourth quarters. They'll have more inventory on hand and be ordering less than they planned. We have to outguess them because we're responsible for our forecast—they aren't.

Figure 5.12 shows the final forecast. This is the result of a combination of customer poll, data analysis, spreadsheet analysis, and educated guessing. Some of the bigger increases are pared down and the final outlook is for another 20%-growth year.

The final version projects total sales for 2011 of 2,834 units, which is 23% more than in 2010. It's still just an educated guess, but at least it is now a good guess, that benefits from the full process of spreadsheet analysis. It takes that general growth rate and those specific customer

◇	A	F	G	H	I	J
1	Cust	Q1-11	Q2-11	Q3-11	Q4-11	FY-2011
2	Smith					
3	Cust A	$35	$45	$60	$38	$178
4	Cust B	$25	$28	$30	$28	$111
5	Cust C	$70	$80	$100	$80	$330
6	Others	$14	$18	$23	$19	$74
7	Smith Total	$144	$171	$213	$165	$693
8	Jones					
9	Cust B	$45	$45	$45	$45	$180
10	Cust D	$55	$65	$75	$70	$265
11	Cust E	$85	$100	$120	$62	$367
12	Cust F	$20	$25	$35	$25	$105
13	Others	$13	$18	$22	$16	$69
14	Jones Total	$218	$253	$297	$218	$986
15	Mitchell					
16	Cust A	$50	$65	$75	$70	$260
17	Cust B	$105	$120	$140	$140	$505
18	Cust E	$42	$52	$56	$47	$197
19	Cust G	$22	$30	$38	$27	$117
20	Others	$17	$19	$23	$17	$76
21	Mitchell Total	$236	$286	$332	$301	$1,155
22	Grand Totals	$598	$710	$842	$684	$2,834
23						
24	Cust A	$85	$110	$135	$108	$438
25	Cust B	$175	$193	$215	$213	$796
26	Cust C	$70	$80	$100	$80	$330
27	Cust D	$55	$65	$75	$70	$265
28	Cust E	$127	$152	$176	$109	$564
29	Cust F	$20	$25	$35	$25	$105
30	Cust G	$22	$30	$38	$27	$117
31	Others	$44	$55	$68	$52	$219
32	Grand Totals	$598	$710	$842	$684	$2,834

Figure 5.12. Final customer poll forecast.

forecasts and merges them in a way that makes good common sense. That common sense factor is the most important, no matter how sophisticated the computer model.

Consolidation

A bottom-up forecast often requires consolidation of several worksheets into a single consolidated worksheet. The better spreadsheets are quite good at this, but there are still some pitfalls to watch for. Please make sure you know how to link worksheets and consolidate in your spreadsheet model.

In a nutshell, linking is easy if your model is small enough that all of the relevant worksheets can be open at the same time. It is considerably more complicated if they cannot all be open at the same time.

Make Your Own

The spreadsheet is meant to handle complicated problems, like a forecast built of several variables. So far our examples have shown sales per customer, salesperson, and region, in a single model or network of related models. We could forecast sales by many finer cuts of information. The imagination is the only limit.

A real forecast might be divided by products to be purchased by each of the customers. Instead of projecting sales for each customer, we could build a forecast of sales to each customer of each product. These could be summed to five a total by customer. Of course, the spreadsheet also allows totaling the sales by product as well. We can also consolidate the product totals across the different customers and different regions, to provide a fully detailed forecast of future sales by product, customer, salesperson, and region.

Add Variables for Detail

This is a reminder from chapter 2, the discussion of breaking things into pieces. We should also add prices to the equation. In that case, the product sales forecasts are done in units, as they have in this chapter, but a separate part of the forecast keeps track of the prices. Once again, the spreadsheet management uses the same logic but with more variables.

Units are summed as before, but the units numbers are multiplied by the price assumptions to produce the final dollar sales figure.

Notice that adding variables to the spreadsheet adds a depth of detail that is useful in several ways. First, it provides additional information. Second—and much more important—we can now track results much more easily. We can track variables, the budgeting buzzword for the difference between what was planned and what actually happened. There is no better way to track these variables than to have finely cut information in the original plan. If, for example, a price changes, it will affect the entire sales forecast. In the spreadsheet forecast that includes product specifics and the price variables, you can simply change the price variable on that product, recalculate, and have all the rest of the forecast change. Salesperson, customer, and regional forecasts all reflect that difference immediately. If you had only the customer totals, salesperson totals, and the regional totals, this would be much more difficult.

CHAPTER 6

S Curves and the Product Life Cycle

Almost all products go through different stages of development, and those stages are reflected in their growth rates. These are shown in Figure 6.1. The important points are at the takeoff and as the market approaches saturation. These are called inflection points.

In the early development stage, growth rates may be high but actual sales are still low. Buyer awareness is just beginning. A few blogs and Web articles describe the new technology. Innovators start to notice the new product. Distribution channels are just beginning to take interest.

By Bob Orsillo via Shutterstock

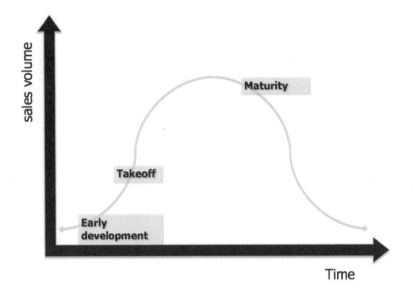

Figure 6.1. Product life cycle.

Then the market takes off. Early buyers have spread the word and the general public begins to follow. This is what happened with so many technology-related items, from televisions to color televisions back in the 20th century, to cell phones, personal computers, multifunction phones, MP3 players, and so many other examples. Those who invested in early stages begin to see profits, growth rates are still attractive, and volumes have skyrocketed. And this phenomenon is not just for high-technology products. Think of organic foods, or low-fat yogurt, or juice bars; and how about gourmet coffee drinks. Lots of markets see take-off phases.

As the market matures, growth rates begin to decline. At this point, most of the buyers who want this product already own it. In the technology areas, often a new technology takes over. Computers get better, laptops get smaller, and multifunction phones and specialty appliances (like MP3 players or video games) move the market. It turns into a lower growth and replacement market, like markets for stoves and refrigerators.

There are three keys to remember when using the product life cycle in your market or sales forecasts:

1. Takeoff starts like a snowball and changes things very quickly. It's hard to overestimate growth at that stage if you happen to hit it big, get buzz, and become one of those special products that captures the market imagination.
2. Once markets are primed, saturation will eventually come too.
3. Each product has a different life cycle; some are faster, some slower, and some quite unlike the normal pattern.

The takeoff is the trickiest. There are markets that never take off at all; some companies spend years waiting in vain for snowballs that never roll. There are also markets that take off at odd moments, not at times you would normally expect, or after long periods of apparent smoldering. The personal digital assistant (PDA) boom was supposed to start back in the early 1990s with the Apple Newton but didn't really until the Palm Pilot came a few years later. Then some would say even that one was eclipsed by the multifunction cell phone. Definitions come into play; sometimes it's hard to tell one product's fade from another product's takeoff. Many businesses go broke waiting for the takeoff, and others change their plans radically, adapting the products to different markets that weren't seen from the beginning. Some revised business plans to adapt, then lost out when the original market appeared. Does this seem too academic? Then think about how this applies to the Web, Web 2.0, and market phenoms like Facebook, MySpace, and LinkedIn.

After takeoff, it's too easy to forget that market growth rates will eventually approach saturation and decline. Telecommunications companies were caught off guard in the early 2000s when the need for connections trailed off. Television manufacturers were anxious for new growth when thin screen and HD technologies put some new boost into the market.

The speed of a life cycle is also hard to predict. The video games industry boomed and faded like a typical fad in the early 1980s, then came back again in the 1990s and again in the new millennium with new product releases like the Wii and Xbox. Personal computers, hard drives for storage, cell phones, and other industries had waves of new technologies to interfere with the basic move to a replacement market. Much depends on exactly what the product does for its buyers and who those buyers are; take your own best guess. Sometimes the standard idea adoption research (see following) will help.

Mature markets are by far the easiest to forecast. These will have slow growth rates and little change from year to year. In these markets, the old-fashioned methods—like taking the average growth rate of the last 5 years and projecting it into the next 5 years—are more likely to work.

Idea Adoption Research

Social scientists have studied adoption of new ideas by many different groups. They have studied how a group of doctors adopt a new treatment technique, how farmers accept a new farming idea, and many other examples of the process of groups of people absorbing innovation.

Most of these studies show a common pattern in adoption of new ideas. They are accepted first by the innovators, who seldom make up more than 2%–3% of the larger group. The innovators prove the idea works, but they have relatively little influence on the group as a whole. The idea takes off when it is taken up by the so-called opinion leaders, who are a second group of roughly 13% of the larger group. These are people smart enough to see what those innovators are doing and influential enough to spread that into the larger group.

This common pattern fits very well with the product life cycle pattern. Figure 6.2 shows how the curve repeats itself with different labels.

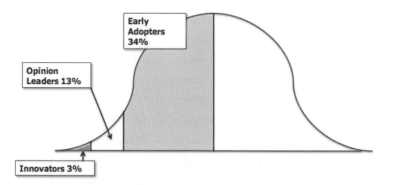

Figure 6.2. Idea adoption.

By Tim Gage via Flickr

Sometimes you can use this research to estimate the speed of the product life cycle. If less than 10% of the potential user group are aware of a new product, then it may still be quite early in the life cycle and there may be a lot of growth left. It may also be ready to take off.

The S Curve in Nature

It's not just sales forecasting. The S curve is a natural phenomenon. It occurs all over nature. If you want an interesting detour, do a Web search for "S curve in nature." Among the things you'll come up with are a lot of interesting photographs, drawings, and this interesting quote from Wikipedia in the entry for *logistic function*. The curve in the figure looks very much like the s curves in previous figures in this chapter. And the explanation includes "The logistic function finds applications in a range of fields, including artificial neural networks, biology, biomathematics, demography, economics, chemistry, mathematical psychology, probability, sociology and statistics." And in nature as well. And it goes on to point out why this happens, which is particularly interesting for business forecasting: "It models the S curve of growth of some set P, where P might be thought of as *population*. The initial stage of growth is approximately exponential; then, as saturation begins, the growth slows, and at maturity, growth stops." Somewhere along the line, in my career,

I realized that almost all markets behave in a way that generates the classic S curve. In the 1980s I developed a software product (no, this isn't a pitch; you can't buy it—it was discontinued years ago) called *Forecaster* that let me draw the curve with a mouse and have the software fill in the numbers. That was because I so often saw the S curve behavior that I wanted to use it without having to do logarithmic equations.

This brings me to the subject of Figure 6.3. This one was done with a simple diffusion model and a spreadsheet. Although there are no complicated equations involved, it does mimic that same behavior of growth within a defined population.

The two curves are both drawn by a spreadsheet with a diffusion model. They show sales of something to a population of 100,000 with a set of assumptions about how people who have it convince the people who don't have it that they ought to.

Did you ever read the Dr. Seuss book about Sneeches? This is like the spreadsheet version of that, and it has real application for forecasting. Let's look at the model.

By Tamako the Jaguar via Flickr

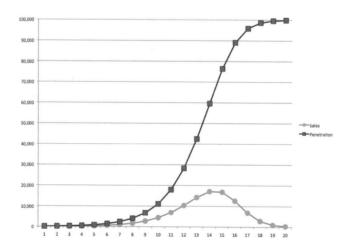

Figure 6.3. Familiar Curves.

Diffusion Model With a Spreadsheet

Diffusion is essentially a buzzword for spreading something through a population. In many ways it's like the spread of a disease, with people who have the disease infecting the people who don't. I once used it very effectively to project the spread of personal computers into Latin America, back in the 1980s. Figure 6.4 shows you the spreadsheet essentials that drew the chart in Figure 6.3.

Please don't be taken aback by the formula in the edit bar in that figure. Suspend disbelief for a minute, if you will, and focus on what's

=IF(B6<Pop,MIN((B6*Factor)*((Pop-B6)/Pop),Pop-B6),0)					
	A	**B**	**C**	**D**	**E**	**F**

◇	A	B	C	D	E	F
1	**Assumptions**					
2	Total population	100,000				
3	Diffusion factor	0.7				
4						
5	**Shipments**	**Installed**		**With Starting Value of 100**		
6	100	100		Factor	Peaks at:	In Year
7	70	170		0.1	2,500	79
8	119	289		0.2	4,997	39
9	201	490		0.3	7,485	28
10	341	832		0.4	9,997	22
11	577	1,409		0.5	12,356	18
12	972	2,381		0.6	14,982	16
13	1,627	4,008		0.7	17,106	14
14	2,693	6,702		0.8	19,884	13
15	4,377	11,079		0.9	22,300	12
16	6,896	17,975		1	24,017	11
17	10,321	28,295		1.25	31,248	10
18	14,202	42,497		1.5	37,443	9
19	17,106	59,603		2	42,801	8
20	16,854	76,458				
21	12,600	89,058				
22	6,821	95,879				
23	2,766	98,645				
24	936	99,581				
25	292	99,873				
26	89	99,962				
27	27	99,989				
28	8	99,997				
29	2	99,999				
30	1	100,000				

Figure 6.4. Spreadsheet diffusion model.

happening in cell A7, where the value showing is 70. At that point, the 100 people who already own the new product influenced 70 of those who didn't. *(And we could call this a disease and an infection process, but this is a book on sales forecasting, so we'll drop that terminology now, leaving it for the epidemiologists.)*

Then look at B7: so the total population of those who had it became 170 during that time.

This brings us to row 8. Those 170 people influenced another 119.

To make sense of that, consider the assumptions above: the population is 100,000 and the diffusion factor is .7. That diffusion factor is how many people who own the new product influence those who don't have it yet to get it. So .7 × 100 is 70, which we see in cell A7. And .7 × 170 is 119, which we see in row 8.

As the installed base grows, however, each owner influences fewer at a time because so many people already own it. If you jump to row 20, the 59,603 owners in row 19 infect only 16,854 in row 20. Simplify those numbers to 60 and 17 and you can see that 17 is not .7 × 60, which should be 42. So cell A20 should show the approximately 60,000 owners influencing about 42,000 people. However, since at that point 60% of the population already has this product, their influence is dampened to about 40% of what it would have been, because only about 40% of the population is left having not bought the new product yet. So the math goes something like this:

$$(59,603 * .7) * ((100,000 - 59,603)/100,000) = 16,854.$$

And that formula is very much like the classic equation for diffusion of anything through a population, as follows:

new sales = owners*(Diffusion factor) * (nonowners/total population).

This, as it turns out, is what's happening with the complicated-looking formula shown in the edit area of Figure 6.4. I'm going to suspend the details for now, leaving them for chapter 10 on spreadsheet fine points, because this is not the place to explain the IF clauses and MIN function. If you can accept that "pop" stands for the value in cell B2 and "factor" stands for the value in B3 (population and diffusion factor, respectively) then you can read the formula there as

$$= (B6 * factor) * ((pop - B6)/pop).$$

And that is a classic diffusion model formula.

Because that might seem a bit esoteric and impractical, I will share here that I used this same model for one of the most accurate sales forecasts I ever did professionally. Apple Computer hired me in 1984 to project sales of personal computers into Latin America. I divided the population into four economic groups, ignored the less advantaged groups because they wouldn't be buying computers, and did two diffusion models for the two highest economic groups. Happily, I was still consulting with Apple Latin America in 1989, when we went back to compare that 1984 forecast to actual results. It turned out to be off by less than 5%.

A More Familiar Forecast Version

You don't need to use a diffusion model to use knowledge of product life cycles and idea adoption patterns in your spreadsheet models for sales and market forecasts. To do that, assume a total potential market for the product you are forecasting and project the installed base for each year as a percentage of the total potential market. Then compare that output with the normal life cycles and the implications of adoption research; in many systems, a graph will help you see the presence of a familiar pattern.

Like other techniques discussed in this book, this one alone will not provide any magical answers. It should be used in conjunction with other analyses and additional information to produce a satisfactory best guess.

However, it is particularly suited to forecasting sales of a brand new product, for which there is no history.

Sample Market-Based Sales Forecast

The market-based sales forecast is most relevant with a new product. The sample market forecast here uses a combination of standard techniques. First, we turn to basic market research to determine the total potential market for this new product. Then we project the gradual increase of installed base, a combination of idea adoption and product life cycle. Finally, we assume new shipments and retirements and project a sales forecast in units, average prices, and market value.

The hypothetical forecast is modeled after classic whole-market forecasts for a new product introduction in a smaller market. It shows the introduction of a new product used in the home, business, and education. For purposes of illustration, we'll call that product a new kind of television/Internet viewer/computer that can display HD television and link to the Web at the same time. It has a large flat screen, a mobile keyboard, and touch remote. We'll call it "NP New" here, for lack of a better name. It's just an example.

Market Segmentation

The sample, like most forecasts, depends on a market segmentation scheme. Segmentation is a framework for dividing a market into different classifications, in this case, users of NP New. The home user is different from the large business user; he or she buys a different product, at a different price, through a different distribution channel. Assumptions are easier to make and future projections easier to understand, when they are broken in to different market segments. This is one of the most important concepts in marketing. The segmentation is often the creative spark for marketing strategy.

Total Potential Market

The market segmentation table show in Figure 6.5 is the result of basic market research. The forecast begins with a determination of the total potential users of the new product. It has to consider demographics, economic trends, buying patterns, use patterns, and other relevant factors. To build this kind of assumption, you consider as much information as you can, and then make an educated guess. How many people will use NP New in their home or business? Here again, you see the importance of the segmentation scheme.

The specific research related to this assumption begins with statistics on total numbers of households, classrooms, businesses, and workers in a

	A	B
1	Penetration	2011
2	Home	500,000
3	Education	750,000
4	Small Business	2,000,000
5	Large Business	500,000
6	Government	1,000,000
7	Whole Market	4,750,000

Figure 6.5. Market segments.

market. When possible, you should be able to segment those households by income level, businesses by size, and workers by job type, education, and other factors. Employment statistics can add information about types of workers and their education and background.

A forecaster modeling total potential market must necessarily make some wide-reaching basic assumptions. You have to assume a price level for the new product, a relationship to substitutes, and certain economic justifications. You have to assume that the total market potential is a stable concept, not changing annually—otherwise you cannot project a gradual increase in penetration. In the real world, the actual level of potential market changes over time. In forecasts, you make do with reasonable assumptions.

Market Penetration

For the next step, find out how many of these products are already installed in this market. This depends far more on good research and intelligent educated guessing than on spreadsheet capabilities. You may be able to find research on the Web. That could be on sale from market research firms, or in press snippets and summaries. For some markets, information has to be generated from primary research, such as user polls and surveys.

Figure 6.6 shows the market penetration table, the result of the sample research for 2011 and the heart of a forecast through 2014. In column B, the worksheet shows estimates of present installed base in each of the

	A	B	C	D	E	F
1	Penetration	2011	2012	2013	2014	2015
2	Home	24,000	37,760	54,382	73,839	97,100
3	Education	35,000	56,650	88,084	134,203	202,861
4	Small Business	66,000	107,350	160,665	229,650	318,908
5	Large Business	72,000	111,480	156,576	208,098	265,815
6	Government	38,000	60,480	88,061	122,538	165,637
7	Whole Market	235,000	373,720	547,768	768,328	1,050,321

Figure 6.6. Market penetration.

user segments. In columns C through E, it shows our estimates of future installed base.

In this case, the forecast of future installed base depends on basic assumptions about product life cycle and idea adoption. We used a combination of inputs:

- The forecast table (shown in Figure 6.8) contains annual shipment estimates by segment. To build these estimates we used the graphics linked to a spreadsheet, developing a graph of estimated values.
- The penetration chart in Figure 6.7 shows the gradual increase of penetration into the total potential market. It mimics the standard S curves we see in real life and past analyses of market penetration, as in Figure 6.1 and 6.2. We use it to evaluate a visual picture of increasing penetration, one that should produce patterns similar to those we see in the product life cycle and idea adoption.
- Retirement estimates, by percent, are shown in Figure 6.9. The project the proportion of NP News in use that will be thrown away or abandoned during a given time period. We need to calculate retirements in order to understand the growth of the total installed base.

These various inputs were compared interactively; that is, we worked on all three items at the same time, in different views of the same spreadsheet, to come out with a final forecast.

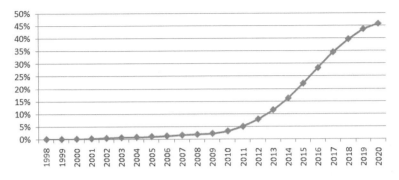

Figure 6.7. Penetration chart.

	A	B	C	D	E	F
9	Shipments	2011	2012	2013	2014	2015
10	Home	12,000	14,000	17,000	20,000	24,000
11	Education	15,000	22,000	32,000	47,000	70,000
12	Small Business	33,000	43,000	56,000	73,000	95,000
13	Large Business	36,000	42,000	49,000	57,000	65,000
14	Government	19,000	24,000	30,000	38,000	48,000
15	Whole Market	115,000	145,000	184,000	235,000	302,000

Figure 6.8. Whole market forecast, units.

The penetration chart, shown in Figure 6.7, was very important. It was made by combining the whole market installed base in the worksheet with estimates for years outside the forecast period, to make an overall picture that makes sense. The graph shows how the forecast assumes gradual penetration of the installed base. Spreadsheet charting was in this case a very important part of the overall forecast because it provided a visual feel for the range of numbers involved.

The annual unit shipment estimates are contained in the same work-sheet. That portion is shown in Figure 6.6. It works in conjunction with the rest of the worksheet to provide installed base numbers that deter-mine the market penetration percent.

The calculation also considers unit retirements. Those assumptions are contained in a separate portion of the worksheet, shown in Figure 6.9.

They are based on market research into retirement patterns for similar products in similar markets.

The formula for installed base combines estimated unit shipments, retirement assumptions, and existing installed base. For example, the formula for the first penetration cell in the segmentation area of the worksheet (cell C2, shown in Figure 6.6) is

$$= B2 + C10 - (B2*C18),$$

where C10 is new shipments to that segment in 2012, shown above in Figure 6.8, and C18 is the retirement percentage assumption for 2012 in that segment, shown Figure 6.7 (following). That formula picks up the installed base from the previous year, adds new shipments for the current year, then subtracts retirements by calculating retirement percentage in the Figure 6.7 multiplied by the previous installed base in the previous column.

The different calculations—installed base, shipments, retirements, total market potential, and market penetration—work together. The spreadsheet uses them to calculate the exact numbers in the appropriate cells and draw the graphs. More importantly, in a forecasting sense, they work together to provide a broad picture of sales into given markets. They all have to make sense together.

Average Prices

A following portion of the sales forecast is reserved for estimated average price or value of the different products in the different user segments. It is shown in Figure 6.8. This is another estimated guess. It is based on

	A	B	C	D	E	F
17	Retirement	2011	2012	2013	2014	2015
18	Home	n.a.	1.0%	1.0%	1.0%	1.0%
19	Education	n.a.	1.0%	1.0%	1.0%	1.0%
20	Small Business	n.a.	2.5%	2.5%	2.5%	2.5%
21	Large Business	n.a.	3.5%	3.5%	3.5%	3.5%
22	Government	n.a.	4.0%	4.0%	4.0%	4.0%

Figure 6.9. Retirement assumptions.

	A	B	C	D	E	F
24	Average price	2011	2012	2013	2014	2015
25	Home	$350	$333	$316	$300	$285
26	Education	$850	$786	$727	$673	$622
27	Small Business	$1,350	$1,316	$1,283	$1,251	$1,220
28	Large Business	$1,550	$1,473	$1,399	$1,329	$1,262
29	Government	$1,600	$1,480	$1,369	$1,266	$1,171

Figure 6.10. Average price forecast.

a combination of market research and subjective judgment, influenced by research into price behavior of similar products in the past and in other markets.

In this case, the forecast assumes declining prices in all the market segments. This is common in electronics products, especially in products related to computing, Internet, and display. Is it right? Who knows? We're guessing the future. Always question the assumptions.

Sales Value

So the value of the sales in this market is at this point a relatively simple calculation. Multiply unit sales by average price for each segment. Spreadsheets are made for this kind of calculation. The result is shown in Figure 6.11.

This is simple multiplication using simple spreadsheet formulas. You should also format the cells for dollars, and manage the units as needed (are these millions or thousands of dollars?). Furthermore, you could easily apply the compound average growth rate (CAGR) calculations we presented in chapters 4 and 8 to provide more information about the forecast.

At this point the sales forecast is complete. For now. We now have projections of total market, penetration, installed base, new unit shipments, retirements, average unit value, and total sales value.

	A	B	C	D	E	F
31	Sales Value	2011	2012	2013	2014	2015
32	Home	$4,200	$4,655	$5,370	$6,002	$6,842
33	Education	$12,750	$17,298	$23,273	$31,619	$43,560
34	Small Business	$44,550	$56,599	$71,867	$91,342	$115,898
35	Large Business	$55,800	$61,845	$68,545	$75,749	$82,061
36	Government	$30,400	$35,520	$41,070	$48,121	$56,225
37	Whole Market	$147,700	$175,916	$210,125	$252,832	$304,586

Figure 6.11. Sales value forecast.

Reality Check

A market forecast should always be subjected to a reality check. If this were a real forecast, we would not finish it without some additional research. We might check production, import, and export figures to see whether our estimates for annual shipments appear to be in the same general range as published figures. We might check with vendors who sold products to this market earlier to see whether their results check with our forecast.

We might also look for macroeconomic data to confirm the relative size of this market compared to other markets with similar characteristics.

CHAPTER 7

Strategic Interactive Model

By jirkaejc via Shutterstock

So far, we have assumed that a sales forecast is a simple guess at future sales. We haven't looked at the impact of our own business decisions, much less those of our competitors. Sales will presumably be higher if we advertise more, higher if we cut our prices (unit sales, at least—although that's a dangerous assumption) and lower if we spend less on Web search terms or advertising, or increase prices (although, again, a dangerous assumption).

Our version of an interactive model is relatively simple, used to make a point. They can be very complicated. Consider the fact that when we increase our own advertising and promotion spending, we also increase the total advertising and promotion spending in the market, which is likely to increase total unit sales. Therefore, our additional unit sales that result from additional spending may not even increase our market share. Furthermore, you could spend a lifetime investigating the exact relationship between advertising, promotion, and price and how they affect sales. Assume that our increase in advertising and our price cut will trigger reactive moves from competitors. You can take profits away from everybody without getting any benefit.

Figure 7.1 show a simple interactive sales forecasting model. Row 4 is a whole market value estimate, presumably something we picked off of the Web from a published forecast, in dollars, not units. Row 5 is an estimated average unit price in the market, which gives us row 6, the market units, by dividing row 4 by row 5. Row 7, called competitive Web spending, estimates what the rest of the market is spending on Web search terms, advertising and banner ads, and any other advertising.

Row 6 uses the spreadsheet Round function, which in this case rounds numbers to the nearest whole number. The formula for B6, for example, is

$$= ROUND((B4*1000)/B5,0).$$

The Round function rounds the product of B4/B5 to the nearest whole number. That rounding function is convenient to simplify your tables; otherwise you have nonsense like fractions of units being sold.

If you wanted to round off a number to a decimal, or to the nearest hundred, you specify that with the number after a comma in the Round function.

$$= ROUND(145,-2)$$

would be 100.

◇	A	B	C	D	E	F
3		2011	2012	2013	2014	2015
4	Market value (thousands)	$350	$700	$1,248	$1,956	$2,640
5	Assumed unit price	$850	$800	$750	$700	$650
6	Whole market units	412	875	1,664	2,794	4,062
7	Competitive web spending	$20,000	$40,000	$150,000	$250,000	$20,000
8	Our price	$825	$775	$725	$700	$650
9	Our web spending	$5,000	$20,000	$100,000	$100,000	$5,000
10	Our unit share %	10%	10.98%	15.81%	19.72%	16.10%
11	Our units	41	96	263	551	654
12	Revenue	$33,825	$74,400	$190,675	$385,700	$425,100
13	Fixed cost	$20,000	$21,000	$22,000	$23,000	$24,000
14	Unit cost	$500.00	$400.00	$250.00	$200.00	$200.00
15	Unit profit	$325	$375	$475	$500	$450
16	Gross profit	13,325	36,000	124,925	275,500	294,300
17	Net before taxes	(11,675)	(5,000)	2,925	152,500	265,300

Figure 7.1. Strategic model.

$$= \text{ROUND}(145.234,1)$$

would be 145.2.

Row 10 in the model makes our unit market share a reflection of our price compared to the market price, our previous year's market share and our Web spending compared to the rest of the market's Web spending. The formula might someday be the result of exhaustive research; some larger companies, generally in the more mature industries, work with models of this sort, produced by comprehensive statistical analysis. In that case, it's another educated guess, used as an illustration only, not presented as the result of solid analysis. The formula for C10 is

$$= (B10 + (B9/(B9 + B7)) + (1 - (B8/B5)))/3.$$

D10 through F10 were produced by copying from C10.

The best way to understand these formulas is to build that model and try it. You'll find that your market share changes one way or another as you change price and advertising strategies.

Market Share and Competition

You can also take the formula apart. It assumes that the present year's market share is the product of three equally weighted factors. The first is B10, the previous year's market share. The second is (B9/(B7 + B9)), which calculates last year's share of total Web spending; if your company's Web spending was a higher share than its market share, then the model says market share will go up. The third phrase (1-(B8/B5)) gives additional market share (or takes it away) for the difference between our price and the average market price. All three share ratings are averaged by dividing their sum by three, as in

(market share + Web spending share + price comparison)/3.

Please remember that there is nothing magic about these formulas: they are simply educated guesses. You can use them as they are, or change them as you wish. They are assumptions—they could be proven or disproven by research, but until then they are interesting mainly for their insight into the interplay between what you spend and what you sell.

The rest of the model reflects our business results as they follow from our marketing strategy. Row 11 converts market share to units, and row 12 converts units to revenue, using our price strategy in row 8. Fixed costs and Web spending are taken into account for a view of eventual profits.

The unit cost in row 14 uses a vertical look-up table. The formula in cell 14B, for example, is

$$= VLOOKUP(B11,\$A\$21:\$B25,2),$$

which is a good example of using the lookup function. That formula looks up the value in B11, then finds the vertical column of the lookup range A21:B25, then picks up the value in the second column of that lookup range. The lookup range is shown in Figure 7.2.

You can see in the figure how the spreadsheet first matches the value in the first column and then picks up the value in the second. So the unit cost in cell B14 of Figure 7.1 is $500, because the spreadsheet looks for 41 in the volume range, finds it between 0 and 50, so picks up $500 in the cost column.

The declining price function might also have been reflected by a simple IF function, such as

$$= IF(B11<200,400,250),$$

which would make the unit cost $400 if the volume were less than 200 units and $350 if the volume were more than 200 units.

◇	A	B
20	Unit Cost Index	
21	0	500
22	50	400
23	100	300
24	250	250
25	500	200

Figure 7.2. Lookup range in the strategic model.

◇	A	B	C	D	E	F
3		2011	2012	2013	2014	2015
4	Market value (thousands)	$350	$700	$1,248	$1,956	$2,640
5	Assumed unit price	$850	$800	$750	$700	$650
6	Whole market units	412	875	1,664	2,794	4,062
7	Competitive web spending	$20,000	$40,000	$150,000	$250,000	$300,000
8	Our price	$750	$725	$675	$700	$650
9	Our web spending	$20,000	$40,000	$150,000	$100,000	$100,000
10	Our unit share %	10%	23.92%	27.77%	29.26%	19.28%
11	Our units	41	209	462	817	783
12	Revenue	$30,750	$151,525	$311,850	$571,900	$508,950
13	Fixed cost	$20,000	$21,000	$22,000	$23,000	$24,000
14	Unit cost	$500.00	$300.00	$250.00	$200.00	$200.00
15	Unit profit	$250	$425	$425	$500	$450
16	Gross profit	10,250	88,825	196,350	408,500	352,350
17	Net before taxes	(29,750)	27,825	24,350	285,500	228,350

Figure 7.3. Scenario 2 of strategic interactive model.

The rest of the model simply takes what we spend and subtracts it from what we make, producing a forecast of profits resulting from different marketing strategies.

Figure 7.3 shows what happens when we change our strategic inputs. You could write this model into your computer and come up with an infinite variety of strategic scenarios, each with their different outputs. Try it.

Remember please that all of this is more art than science. Don't copy my model here unless it fits your situation: Make it your own. There is no prescribed way to do it, except using as much information as possible and a lot of guessing. Try to combine different methods into one forecast and compare the results. Just keep trying until the forecast feels right.

CHAPTER 8

Technical Analysis

I'm not big on technical analysis. I use it to provide an occasional new input or extra insight to forecasts that I believe should depend much more on good research combined with common sense and subjective judgment. We believe that technical tools will rarely be as valuable as simpler and less mathematical approaches. Furthermore, I think they are dangerous because they can hide mediocre work. Just as fancy presentation techniques can make poor forecasts look good, fancy statistical techniques can make poor forecasting sound good.

We include these technical tools, however, for two good reasons. First, when used well, they provide valuable additional input and a reality check on other forecasting methods. They can stimulate thought and provide a useful background for the educated guess. Second, the terms involved are part of forecasting jargon; we want to explain them and provide examples so you will recognize their value and their limits.

By Tischenko Irina via Shutterstock

This is a quick treatment of some very sophisticated topics. Please look elsewhere for more depth. We want merely to familiarize you with some basic terms and simple tricks so that you can use them in a practical context and understand them when others make reference to them.

The statistical analysis tools suffer from an inherent weakness. They all work on the basic premise that the past predicts the future. Sometimes it does, but not always. These tools are best used as a means to provide extra input to the subjective, educated guess process. Generate all the statistical analysis first, consider the different results you get and only then make the final forecast.

Averages and Smoothing

Averages and smoothing are easy to understand and simple to put into spreadsheet terms. We offer two quick examples for curiosity value. As a minor input to a forecasting problem, not a solution, they can be useful.

Simple Moving Average

The simple moving average follows a forecast through its changes. In the worksheet shown in Figure 8.1, we use a moving average to calculate each new month as the average of the past three months.

The moving-average formula for a 3-month moving average is

Forecast = (last month + 2 months ago + 3 months ago)/3.

Therefore, the formula in cell B6, for example, is

$$= SUM(C3:G5)/3.$$

This provides an estimate of future sales, on a month-by-month basis, as shown in the chart in Figure 8.2. Notice how the forecast line tracks the actual sales line.

Using the same data in Figure 8.1, we can calculate a simple moving average for the month of January, using 3-month, 6-month, and 12-month moving averages. There is a significant difference between the three averages. The first is calculated as above. The second sums the

	A	B	C	D
1	Month	Forecast	Sales	Difference
2	Nov	n.a	280	n.a
3	Dec	n.a	350	n.a
4	Jan	n.a	180	n.a
5	Feb	270	250	20
6	Mar	260	330	70
7	Apr	253	370	117
8	May	317	280	37
9	Jun	327	320	7
10	Jul	323	290	33
11	Aug	297	275	22
12	Sep	295	320	25
13	Oct	295	345	50
14	Nov	313	360	47
15	Dec	342	410	68
16	Jan	372		

Figure 8.1. Simple moving average.

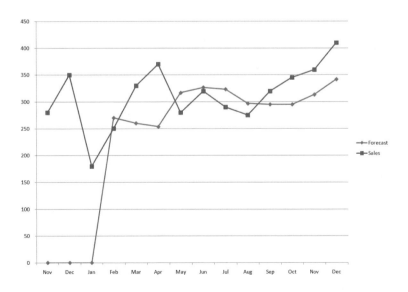

Figure 8.2. Moving average lines.

previous six months and divides by six. The third sums the previous 12 months and divides by twelve. The results are summarized in Figure 8.3.

These averages should be applied, if at all, with common sense. There should be some logical reason for using the last 3 months or the last 12 months, or whatever period you choose.

Weighted Moving Average

The weighted moving average is a sophistication of the simple moving average. Different months have different weights and the weights are determined through some logical method. For example, you might combine a moving average with a weighting system that relates to seasonal changes. There's a simple example in Figure 8.4.

The example improves on the simple moving average by paying more respect to the seasonal importance of sales of 12 months earlier. To build such a system, first set your own weights, multiply the data by its weight, and then sum the result, as shown in the figure. The sum of the weights should be 1, just as in Figure 8.4.

Exponential Smoothing

Exponential smoothing is an arbitrary method for smoothing past data to correct for what appears to be random swings upward and downward. It requires comparison of past sales and forecast data, which is multiplied according to some arbitrary number, usually called an alpha value, to calculate an ongoing forecast. Alpha normally falls between 0 and 1.

The smooth chart in Figure 8.5 shows the result. The forecast falls between the swings of the real data.

	A	B
19	Simple average	
20	Last 3 months	371.7
21	Last 6 months	333.3
22	Last 12 months'	310.8

Figure 8.3. Averaging examples.

	A	B	C	D
24	Weighted Average			
25	Month	Weight	Value	
26	Oct	25%	345	86.25
27	Nov	30%	360	108
28	Dec	20%	410	82
29	Jan	25%	180	45
30			Forecast:	321.25

Figure 8.4. Weighted moving average.

The Figure 8.5 worksheet uses exponential smoothing to forecast sales from past sales and past forecasts. It is an example of the smoothing formula, which in general terms, assuming some arbitrary alpha value, is

Feb forecast = (1-alpha) * Jan forecast + alpha * Jan sales.

We apply that formula in the worksheet in Figure 8.6, in the forecast data in column B. Cell B4, for example, contains the formula

$$= (1 - \$B\$19)*B3 + (\$B\$19*C3),$$

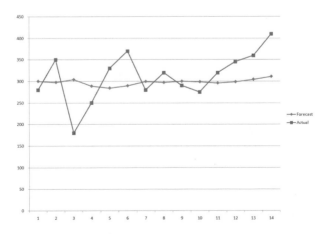

Figure 8.5. Smoothing lines chart.

	A	B	C	D
1	Month	Forecast	Sales	Difference
2	Nov	300	280	n.a
3	Dec	298	350	52
4	Jan	304	180	124
5	Feb	289	250	39
6	Mar	284	330	46
7	Apr	290	370	80
8	May	299	280	19
9	Jun	297	320	23
10	Jul	300	290	10
11	Aug	299	275	24
12	Sep	296	320	24
13	Oct	299	345	46
14	Nov	304	360	56
15	Dec	311	410	99
16	Jan	323		
17				
18	Alpha	0.12	Sum of difference	
19	Growth			642.195

Figure 8.6. Exponential smoothing worksheet.

where B19 is the arbitrary alpha value, B3 is the previous forecast, and C3 is the previous month's sales.

What good is exponential smoothing? The graph in Figure 8.5 shows how it smooths the extremes and offers an average path through the hills and valleys. That can help a forecast when it is used in combination with other techniques and with common sense and judgment.

Regression and Correlation

Sometimes two sets of numbers move up or down together in some recognizable order. Most people expect production to increase when investment increases, and the stock market index usually increases when interest rates decrease. Tire sales usually increase when auto sales increase, because a large share of the tire makers' volume goes onto new cars. This relationship is called correlation. One row of data correlates with another: they move up, or down, together.

Sometimes correlation works in reverse. In most markets, volume increases when price decreases, and vice versa. The stock market index usually goes down when interest rates go up, and vice versa. These relationships are called negative correlation, and can be just as valuable as positive correlation.

Trend Analysis

Trend analysis looks for correlation between time periods and some other data, such as sales. A trend analysis looks for a pattern of sales growth or sales decline over time.

Regression Analysis

Regression analysis explores relationships between different sets of data and projects those relationships from past into the future. When a regression is successful it produces a formula that relates one row of data to another; the measure of that success is also called correlation. When data are highly correlated, regression produces a useful equation that relates one row to another. If not, regression is of little use. Statistical analysis tools include ways to measure and compare correlations.

Regression and correlation are usually complicated analyses. In their most sophisticated versions, they are the foundations of complex econometric models made up of thousands of equations and variables. People spend years studying these relationships and ways to manage information based on them

We don't get complicated here. Simple correlations can help you forecast. The market share model is a correlation forecast: it makes sales equal to the whole market times some percentage number. Many other simple uses of correlation can be valuable in sales forecasting.

The main idea is finding some easily available number that leads to a more difficult number. The best example is when a readily available whole-market forecast leads you to a company sales forecast like the market share model. Whole-market forecasts are usually available in business magazines and from trade associations and research firms.

Figure 8.7 shows a sample regression forecast worksheet developed with the single regression worksheet. It shows a simple example of statistical forecasting. It uses some whole-market indicators and some related products to understand what goes on with product ABC.

The first part of the worksheet, the data for the years 2006 through 2010, is based on history. There we see how Product ABC sales have performed in the past and how industry sales, widget sales, and one expert forecaster have performed. Industry sales and widget sales are historical, and the expert's row is what she predicted would happen to industry sales before the fact.

	A	B	C	D	E	F
1		2006	2007	2008	2009	2010
2	Year	1	2	3	4	5
3	Product ABC Sales	312	455	543	470	455
4	Industry Sales	4,320	5,560	6,800	5,750	5,200
5	Widget Sales	2,020	1,600	1,350	1,450	1,835
6	Expert Forecast	4,000	5,500	6,250	5,500	5,250
7	ABC/Industry	7.22%	8.18%	7.99%	8.17%	8.75%
8	ABC/Widget	15.45%	28.44%	40.22%	32.41%	24.80%
9						
10	Regression: (y=mx + b)	Slope	Intercept	Rsquared		
11	Year	30.1	356.70	32.24%		
12	Industry sales	0.09	(44.82)	91.20%		
13	Widget sales	(0.27)	894.36	79.34%		
14	Expert Forecast	0.10	(92.91)	98.79%		
15						
16	Forecasts	2011	2012	2013		
17	Year	6	7	8		
18	Industry Sales	5,000	5,500	6,000		
19	Widget Sales	1,400	1,200	1,050		
20	Expert Forecast	5,250	6,000	7,000		
21						
22	Product ABC Forecasts	2011	2012	2013	CAGR	
23	Straight-line time series	537	567	598	9.51%	
24	Industry-based	400	445	489	2.44%	
25	Widget-based	515	569	610	10.26%	
26	Expert-based	442	518	620	10.88%	

Figure 8.7. Sample regression analysis.

There are some apparent patterns. Product ABC sales come to about 7% or 8% of the whole market, and they obviously go up when the market goes up, and down when it goes down. They seem to move in reverse of the widget sales—when widgets go down, ABC goes up, and vice versa. The forecaster is close to industry sales, but tends to underestimate. In 2008 she overestimated though, so maybe she's noticed now and is compensating for the earlier misses.

The chart in Figure 8.8 shows the apparent relationship between the different indicators. It shows how the ABC sales seemed to move in the same direction as the industry sales and the expert forecast.

We want to get at those patterns somehow, to use them for our forecast. One simple way shows up in rows 7 and 8 of the worksheet in which we divide our sales by industry sales, and then by widget sales. In the first division we find our 7%–8% market share coming out. In the second, we don't seem to have a helpful pattern, despite the way the widgets and ABC move in reverse.

Statistical analysis offers more sophisticated, formal, and measurable tools for exploring the data. The result of simple regression is a mathematical equation that relates one set of numbers to the other. That formula can be stated in several ways, all of which mean the same thing:

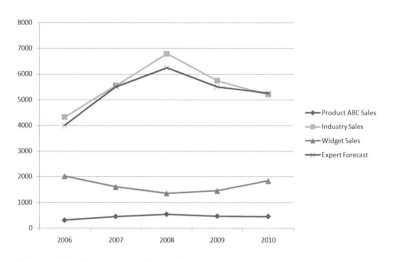

Figure 8.8. Regression data plot.

$$FORECAST = CONSTANT\ NUMBER + (SLOPE * INDICATOR)$$

or

$$Y = K + M*X$$

or

$$= INTERCEPT + (SLOPE * INDICATOR)$$

or

$$A = mB + C.$$

The regression analysis sample in this chapter gives us equations to relate ABC sales to other indicators. The equations can be expressed in the form

$$ABC = C + (B*Indicator),$$

where C is in column C and B is in column B. For example, according to the numbers in row 24 of Figure 8.8:

$$ABC = -44.82 + (.09*Industry\ sales).$$

In row 25, we have

$$ABC = 894 - (0.27 * Widget\ Sales)$$

and so forth. The straight tie series assumes some spreadsheet default treatment, which we will explain later.

These equations can be very useful. If we have a good forecast of industry sales or widgets, or if we trust the expert forecast, then we can use those and relate our ABC sales to them by means of the equations. In rows 21–25 of the sample worksheet in Figure 8.7, we did exactly that. We took available forecasts for the industry, for widgets, and by our favorite expert, and used them to project our ABC sales according to the regression equations. That produced the results shown in that figure.

Now we need to measure correlation to distinguish between different forecasts. We have four competing forecasts, each based on statistical analysis of past trends. To determine which might be more useful, turn to the correlation numbers in column D of rows 11–14.

These numbers were produced by a standard spreadsheet function, which measures correlation according to the standard "R?" method. For the statistical formulas behind R?, you will have to refer to a more detailed source of information. For our purposes, the R? function we added to the spreadsheet produces an R? number that is the standard for measurement of degree of correlation in this kind of statistical analysis. The closer this number is to 1 (for 100%), the farther from 0, the better the correlation. In the real world, R? readings of 70% and 80% are consider unusually good, and an R? of 90% or better is quite unusual, almost unnatural. Ours is unnatural because we tailored the data.

The correlation is measured in the past. The mathematical formula calculates theoretical ABC sales based on the equation, and the difference between the theoretical, equation-based values for 1986–1990, and the real values. Presumably—although there is no guarantee—high correlation in the past means high correlation in the future. This is, of course, a rather questionable assumption, but you have to examine that one yourself because the analytical techniques ignore it.

The correlation readings show us that the expert forecast is the best measure. During the 1988–1992 period, our sales were highly correlated with what the expert said. Industry sales were also highly correlated, widget sales less so, and the straight time series was not correlated at all. Regress 2 in Figure 8.9 shows graphically what the correlation measure tells us mathematically.

The chart plots the actual past sales against the theoretical values produced by the linear regression equations. It shows how close the equation based on the expert was, and how far off the time series was.

The time series analysis in row 11 is a special case linear regression. In this case, the independent variable, or forecast indicator, is a simple number corresponding to the column sequence. The year 2006 is 1, 2007 is 2, and so on.

The result is the simple time trend equation produced in row 11, and the low correlation. The line chart in Figure 8.9 shows how the time

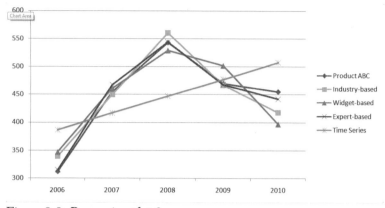

Figure 8.9. Regression plot 2.

series draws a single straight line through the very curvy line of actual sales data for product ABC.

So now we have four competing forecasts. We have to choose among these four or produce a fifth. Once again we're in the judgment phase of a forecast. After assimilating different sources of information, the last step is to apply common sense to produce the final forecast. In this case we would probably use the expert forecast version, because it looks like the best reflection of a low growth 1991. Both the industry association and the expert expect low growth in that year, and the expert's formula comes close to that. It also falls between the other two. Better still, though, we end up building our own forecast (shown in Figure 8.10) that takes the best from the different formulas and comes up with an intermediate forecast in between them the two extremes. The final forecast also has the advantage of looking as unscientific as it is. It's better that way.

A	B	C	D	E
22 Product ABC Forecasts	2011	2012	2013	CAGR
23 Straight-line time series	537	567	598	9.51%
24 Industry-based	400	445	489	2.44%
25 Widget-based	515	569	610	10.26%
26 Expert-based	442	518	620	10.88%
27 Final Forecast	450	525	600	9.66%

Figure 8.10. Final forecast.

Forecasting summary: Remember that all of this is more art than science. Don't copy anybody else's model unless it fits well: make it your own. There is no single right way to do it, except using as much information as possible and a lot of guessing, Try to combine different methods into one forecast and compare the results.

CHAPTER 9

Managing a Forecast

As I wrote in chapter 1, sales forecasting is about management. A forecast without follow-up tracking and management is a waste of time.

It's More About People Than Numbers

Don't get caught forgetting what a sales forecast is for. It's to help you manage your company. To make it worth the trouble, you want to involve all of the people who will be charged with making things happen. Don't ever impose a sales forecast on people who haven't had a chance to contribute to the process. The first thing they are going to do, if troubles arise, is doubt the credibility of the forecast.

Even if it's just you, starting a new company, with no partners or investors or team members, don't forget that the forecasting is about managing. You want to be able to steer your company with the difference between plan and actual.

By Dusty Cline, istockphoto.com (modified)

In all cases, avoid what I call the "crystal ball and chain" problem. That's when people object to a forecast because it's setting down numbers that they fear will be used against them. Good management doesn't let that happen. The forecast is collaborative. As time moves forward, if actual results are worse than the forecast, management has to stay collaborative to develop course corrections.

Start With a Realistic Forecast

Don't confuse sales forecasting with sales management or employee incentives or carrots or sticks. I've seen that done too often. One of my otherwise-favorite clients would routinely publish a sales forecast about 1.5 or 2 times greater than any realistic number that anybody would believe in. He'd pretend it was the real target. I was in one meeting with him where he had all of the channel managers, sales managers, and distributors take turns signing a big page on an easel with a forecast of $60 million. Every one of them signed but every one of them also knew $35 or maybe $40 million was the best they could do.

I talked to him about it many times. I said an unrealistic forecast worked against his management team. It hurt credibility. He insisted that he liked it that way, but we also kept two sets of sales forecast

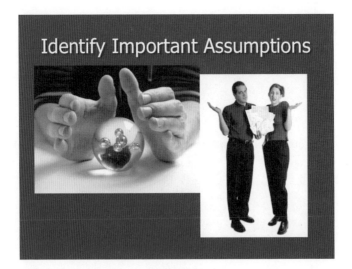

By Neils Lan, Sharon Dominick, istockphoto.com

numbers: the unrealistically high forecast we shared with the sales team in the group and a realistic lower number that was passed upward to corporate management.

Make the Assumptions Specific

You've seen a lot of assumptions laid out in the various sample forecasts and examples in this book. That started with assumptions like the restaurant capacity-based assumptions and the Web traffic assumptions in chapter 2, then lots of explicit assumptions in the following chapters.

Listing the assumptions makes a big difference as you manage the forecast. All forecasts will be wrong, which doesn't mean they aren't vital management tools; but it does mean that you want to assume every forecast will need regular course corrections. And for that you want to keep track of assumptions so you can keep track of what's changed.

Set the Review Schedule

The first step in good forecasting is to set a review schedule with the managers in charge. That means a regular review, something like the third Thursday of every month, for example. Everybody involved should know when the monthly reviews are scheduled. These are important meetings.

Track Results Carefully

In chapter 2 we presented Magda's sales forecast, as shown in Figure 9.1.

With that in mind, let's look at the actual sales results in Figure 9.2.

And with that, we can calculate the difference between plan and actual, which is called the *variance*. That's shown in Figure 9.3.

So it's worth noting there are some fine points in correct accounting of variance, as shown in this figure:

- In sales units, price, and sales value, amounts greater than planned are a positive variance and amounts less than planned are a negative variance. So the value for lunch units in January is negative because Magda planned on 119 but only sold 61, which is 58 less than planned. So it's a negative 58 variance.

	A	C	D	E
16	**Sales Forecast**			
17		Jan	Feb	Mar
18	**Unit Sales**			
19	Lunches	119	227	302
20	Lunch Bvg	119	227	302
21	Dinners	500	600	728
22	Dinner Bvg	500	454	604
23	Other	50	83	103
24	**Total Unit Sales**	1,288	1,591	2,039
25				
26	**Unit Prices**	Jan	Feb	Mar
27	Lunches	$10.00	$10.00	$10.00
28	Lunch Bvg	$2.00	$2.00	$2.00
29	Dinners	$20.00	$20.00	$20.00
30	Dinner Bvg	$4.00	$4.00	$4.00
31	Other	$10.00	$10.00	$10.00
32				
33	**Sales**			
34	Lunches	$1,190	$2,270	$3,020
35	Lunch Bvg	$238	$454	$604
36	Dinners	$10,000	$12,000	$14,560
37	Dinner Bvg	$2,000	$1,816	$2,416
38	Other	$500	$830	$1,030
39	**Total Sales**	$13,928	$17,370	$21,630
40				
41	**Direct Unit Costs**	Jan	Feb	Mar
42	Lunches	$2.50	$2.50	$2.50
43	Lunch Bvg	$0.30	$0.30	$0.30
44	Dinners	$7.00	$7.00	$7.00
45	Dinner Bvg	$0.80	$0.80	$0.80
46	Other	$4.00	$4.00	$4.00
47				
48	**Direct Cost of Sales**			
49	Lunches	$298	$568	$755
50	Lunch Bvg	$36	$68	$91
51	Dinners	$3,500	$4,200	$5,096
52	Dinner Bvg	$400	$363	$483
53	Other	$200	$332	$412
54	**Subtotal Direct Cost**	$4,433	$5,531	$6,837

Figure 9.1. The sales forecast.

And the value for lunch units in March is positive 39, sales of 341 compared to planned sales of 302.

- In costs, amounts less than planned are positive and amounts more than planned are negative variance. So the unit cost of lunches has a negative variance for January because it was supposed to be $2.50 per lunch and it ended up as $3.41 per lunch, $0.91 more. And in the direct cost of lunches there was

Actual Sales				
	Jan	Feb	Mar	A
Unit Sales				
Lunches	61	175	341	38
Lunch Bvg	88	174	245	2€
Dinners	590	703	800	746
Dinner Bvg	567	566	622	70
Other	77	67	65	6
Total Unit Sales	1,383	1,686	2,073	2,17
Unit Prices	Jan	Feb	Mar	Ap
Lunches	$13.41	$9.22	$9.94	$9.77
Lunch Bvg	$1.68	$1.56	$1.48	$1.63
Dinners	$22.79	$21.91	$22.06	$24.13
Dinner Bvg	$4.27	$4.65	$4.90	$4.7
Other	$9.76	$10.43	$12.01	$11.
Sales				
Lunches	$818	$1,613	$3,392	$3,76
Lunch Bvg	$148	$273	$363	$46
Dinners	$13,433	$15,403	$17,642	$18,000
Dinner Bvg	$2,420	$2,629	$3,047	$3,3
Other	$755	$700	$777	$711
Total Sales	$17,574	$20,618	$25,221	$26,27€
Direct Unit Costs	Jan	Feb	Mar	
Lunches	$3.41	$2.34	$1.83	$1.55
Lunch Bvg	$0.51	$0.46	$0.43	$0.40
Dinners	$5.02	$5.05	$5.44	$5.38
Dinner Bvg	$0.63	$0.55	$0.68	$0.6€
Other	$2.11	$4.39	$5.55	$5.4
Direct Cost of Sales				
Lunches	$208	$410	$624	$59
Lunch Bvg	$45	$81	$105	$11
Dinners	$2,961	$3,547	$4,349	$4,0
Dinner Bvg	$359	$313	$421	$47
Other	$163	$295	$359	$34
Subtotal Direct Cost	$3,736	$4,646	$5,858	$5,5

Figure 9.2. Actual Sales Results.

Sales Variance	Jan	Feb	Mar	
Unit Sales				
Lunches	-58	-52	39	
Lunch Bvg	-31	-53	-57	
Dinners	90	103	72	
Dinner Bvg	67	112	18	
Other	27	-16	-38	
Total Unit Sales	95	95	34	
Unit Prices	Jan	Feb	Mar	
Lunches	$3.41	($0.78)	($0.06)	(
Lunch Bvg	($0.32)	($0.44)	($0.52)	
Dinners	$2.79	$1.91	$2.06	$.
Dinner Bvg	$0.27	$0.65	$0.90	
Other	($0.24)	$0.43	$2.01	
Sales				
Lunches	($372)	($657)	$372	
Lunch Bvg	($90)	($181)	($241)	
Dinners	$3,433	$3,403	$3,082	$4
Dinner Bvg	$420	$813	$631	
Other	$255	($130)	($253)	
Total Sales	$3,646	$3,248	$3,591	$
Direct Unit Costs	Jan	Feb	Mar	
Lunches	($0.91)	$0.16	$0.67	
Lunch Bvg	($0.21)	($0.16)	($0.13)	($
Dinners	$1.98	$1.95	$1.56	
Dinner Bvg	$0.17	$0.25	$0.12	
Other	$1.89	($0.39)	($1.55)	(
Direct Cost of Sales				
Lunches	$90	$158	$131	
Lunch Bvg	($9)	($13)	($14)	
Dinners	$539	$653	$747	$
Dinner Bvg	$41	$50	$62	
Other	$37	$37	$53	
Subtotal Direct Cost d	$697	$885	$979	

Figure 9.3. The variance.

a positive variance of $90 because the total of only $208 is $90 less than the planned $298.

- Positive variance isn't always good news. The positive variance in the direct cost of lunches, for example, was just a disappointing result of selling much fewer lunches than planned.
- Negative variance isn't always bad news. We don't have an immediate example in these results, but sometimes total costs can be above plan because total sales are above plan.

Variance isn't about the numbers; it's about the management. You should look into the variance to identify real causes. Have assumptions changed? Have plans been implemented?

Where sales are better than expected, you want to know why and how you can take advantage of whatever is the cause. Happily, in this case, Magda's new restaurant is selling even better than its plan and that's the second plan, the more optimistic of the two. Dinners are going very well, above plan in sales and below plan in cost of sales per dinner.

Do you adjust your plan? Here again, it's about people, talking, examining the situation behind the numbers. If it were me, just from what we see here, I might adjust the plan to make sales of lunches lower and sales of dinners higher.

CHAPTER 10

Spreadsheet Tips and Traps

It's not that the subject of this book is spreadsheet work, rather than sales forecasting. However, since the daily work and nuts and bolts of sales forecasting tends to be with spreadsheets, it's hard to imagine this book without this chapter. Let's look at some specific spreadsheet fine points that will help. I'm going to try to put this in the same order these fine points appeared in the book, by referencing the figures in which they first come up.

Referencing an Entire Row With a Single Cell

This comes up first in Figure 2.2, showing a simple sales forecast including units and price per unit. I use it a lot. I'm lazy, so I like to set up my spreadsheet to automatically repeat the price I type into the leftmost column. In Figure 10.1, you can see in the formula edit bar how cell C11 automatically picks up whatever I type into B11. Its formula is

$$= B11.$$

If you could see the formulas, you'd see that the same kind of simple price trigger is set up in all of the price cells except the ones in the

=B11					
◇	A	B	C	D	E
10	**Unit Prices**	Jan	Feb	Mar	Apr
11	Lunches	$7.00	$7.00	$7.00	$7.00
12	Dinners	$14.50	$14.50	$14.50	$14.50
13	Drinks	$3.50	$3.50	$3.50	$3.50
14	Other	$15.00	$15.00	$15.00	$15.00

Figure 10.1. Flowing values to the right.

leftmost column, for the first month. Each cell in the price assumptions, from February to December, picks up the value in the cell to its left.

That saves me typing. When I change a price in January, if I do nothing else, I change that same price for the whole worksheet.

This doesn't mean I have to keep the same price throughout the forecast. I can change any of those assumptions by just typing in a new price. But if I don't, and I leave the prices stable, I only have to type it once, into the first cell in the row.

Calculating Average Prices

Also in chapter 2, in the next figure, we came across the relatively complicated formula shown in the edit bar in Figure 10.2 (which is identical to Figure 2.3, but repeated here to save you having to turn back the pages). That formula is

$$= IF(N5<>0,N18/N5,0).$$

	O12	▾	f_x =IF(O5<>0,O18/O5,0)					
	A	B	C	D	M	N	O	
1	Sales Forecast							
2			Jan	Feb	Nov	Dec	2010	
3	Unit Sales							
4	Lunches	10%	200	220	403	443	3,594	
5	Dinners	5%	450	473	608	638	6,466	
6	Drinks	75%	488	520	758	811	7,545	
7	Other		50	60	150	160	1,260	
8	Total Unit Sales		1,188	1,273	1,919	2,052	18,865	
9								
10	Unit Prices		Jan	Feb	Nov	Dec	2010	
11	Lunches		$6.00	$6.50	$7.00	$7.50	$6.65	
12	Dinners		$13.00	$13.00	$16.00	$17.00	$13.93	
13	Drinks		$2.00	$3.00	$3.00	$3.00	$2.72	
14	Other		$13.00	$14.00	$15.00	$15.00	$14.21	
15								
16	Sales							
17	Lunches		$1,200	$1,430	$2,821	$3,323	$23,906	
18	Dinners		$5,850	$6,149	$9,728	$10,846	$90,084	
19	Drinks		$975	$1,560	$2,274	$2,433	$20,553	
20	Other		$650	$840	$2,250	$2,400	$17,900	
21	Total Sales		$8,675	$9,979	$17,073	$19,002	$152,442	

Figure 10.2. Repeat of 2.3, average prices.

So that brings up several reasonable questions. Why the IF clause, and why the division? Why not just pick up the price from the previous cell? Or take the average of the prices in the monthly cells?

The answer becomes clearer when we have changing pricing during the course of the year, which is almost always the real case. Consider Figure 10.3, which is based on Magda's new restaurant forecast shown in Figure 2.6, but with the added subtlety of changing prices.

Now suddenly there's a difference. The formula shown in the edit bar, the equivalent to the same formula in Figures 10.1 and 2.3 but moved one column to the right (because Magda, in chapter 2, inserted a column B for keeping assumptions, between Figure 2.3 and doing her final forecast, from which this one is taken), is correct. You can check it by taking the $90,084 sales in cell O18 and dividing that number by the 6,466 units in cell O5. The product will be the average price, $13.93. Try it with a calculator.

So let's look at why it has to be this more complicated formula, by examining two simpler ones, and what's wrong with them.

=IF(O5<>0,O18/O5,0)							
◇	A	B	C	D	M	N	O	P
1	**Sales Forecast**							
2			Jan	Feb	Nov	Dec	2010	
3	**Unit Sales**							
4	Lunches	10%	200	220	403	443	3,594	4,
5	Dinners	5%	450	473	608	638	6,466	9,
6	Drinks	75%	488	520	758	811	7,545	10,
7	Other		50	60	150	160	1,260	1,
8	**Total Unit Sales**		1,188	1,273	1,919	2,052	18,865	25,
9								
10	**Unit Prices**		Jan	Feb	Nov	Dec	2010	
11	Lunches		$6.00	$6.50	$7.00	$7.50	$6.65	$6
12	Dinners		$13.00	$13.00	$16.00	$17.00	$13.93	$13
13	Drinks		$2.00	$3.00	$3.00	$3.00	$2.72	$2
14	Other		$13.00	$14.00	$15.00	$15.00	$14.21	$14
15								
16	**Sales**							
17	Lunches		$1,200	$1,430	$2,821	$3,323	$23,906	$31,
18	Dinners		$5,850	$6,149	$9,728	$10,846	$90,084	$125,
19	Drinks		$975	$1,560	$2,274	$2,433	$20,553	$28,
20	Other		$650	$840	$2,250	$2,400	$17,900	$21,
21	Total Sales							

Figure 10.3. With changing price assumptions.

The Average Price Error

This formula is a classic application of spreadsheet IF logic (see below) and the right calculation of the average price, avoiding several common errors.

The first of these common errors is the simple average price error. Consider the sample in Figure 10.4.

Not much difference between $13.83, the value in this version for O12 and $13.93, the correct value. Sure. But imagine yourself presenting your sales forecast to boss, owner, partner, banker, or investor…probably nobody would notice, but how would you feel if somebody took a calculator, did the math, and discovered your numbers were off?

The formula for cell O12, where $13.83 is the value, is

$$= Average(C12:N12),$$

which seems logical, but isn't correct.

If that's too subtle, consider the case in Figure 10.5. In this case the formula (not shown) for cell F3 is

$$= Average(B3:E3).$$

fx	=AVERAGE(C12:N12)							
◇	A	C	G	K	L	M	N	O
1	Sales Forecast							
2		Jan	May	Sep	Oct	Nov	Dec	2010
3	Unit Sales							
4	Lunches	200	293	333	366	403	443	3,594
5	Dinners	450	548	551	579	608	638	6,466
6	Drinks	488	631	663	709	758	811	7,545
7	Other	50	90	130	140	150	160	1,260
8	Total Unit Sa	1,188	1,562	1,677	1,794	1,919	2,052	18,865
9								
10	Unit Prices	Jan	May	Sep	Oct	Nov	Dec	2010
11	Lunches	$6.00	$6.50	$6.50	$6.50	$7.00	$7.50	$6.65
12	Dinners	$13.00	$13.50	$13.00	$14.00	$16.00	$17.00	$13.83
13	Drinks	$2.00	$3.00	$2.50	$2.50	$3.00	$3.00	$2.72
14	Other	$13.00	$14.00	$14.00	$14.00	$15.00	$15.00	$14.21
15								
16	Sales							
17	Lunches	$1,200	$1,905	$2,165	$2,379	$2,821	$3,323	$23,906
18	Dinners	$5,850	$7,398	$7,163	$8,106	$9,728	$10,846	$90,084
19	Drinks	$975	$1,893	$1,658	$1,773	$2,274	$2,433	$20,553

Figure 10.4. Average price error example.

◇	A	B	C	D	E	F
1		Month1	Month2	Month3	Month4	Total
2	Units	100	1,100	2,250	3,500	6,950
3	Price	$10.00	$5.00	$2.00	$1.00	$4.50
4	Sales	$1,000	$5,500	$4,500	$3,500	$14,500

Figure 10.5. Dumb-looking average error.

The spreadsheet calculates that correctly, adding up the sum of the values in the cells (10+5+2+1 = 18) and dividing by 4, showing $4.50. And if you left that value, $4.50, in cell O12 instead of the correct value, you'd have a dumb-looking spreadsheet. It would appear to be multiplying 6,950 by $4.50 and getting $14,500 as a result. Put that into your spreadsheet and you open yourself up to a very embarrassing situation when somebody reading your work points out that

$$6,950 * 4.50 = 31,275$$

...and your spreadsheet seems to indicate that the basic math is wrong.

So you want to avoid that error. Don't process the average price wrong.

The Most Recent Price Error

You also want to avoid using the most recent price. For example, go back to Figure 10.1 or Figure 10.2 and imagine the formula for cell O12 as

$$= N12.$$

That could also seem logical, but the value in N12 is $17.00, not $13.83, so that would produce another dumb-looking spreadsheet error. It's more obvious with the simpler version in Figure 10.6.

◇	A	B	C	D	E	F
1		Month1	Month2	Month3	Month4	Total
2	Units	100	1,100	2,250	3,500	6,950
3	Price	$10.00	$5.00	$2.00	$1.00	$1.00
4	Sales	$1,000	$5,500	$4,500	$3,500	$14,500

Figure 10.6. Another dumb-looking price display error.

F3		fx =F4/F2				
◇	A	B	C	D	E	F
1		Month1	Month2	Month3	Month4	Total
2	Units	100	1,100	2,250	3,500	6,950
3	Price	$10.00	$5.00	$2.00	$1.00	$2.09
4	Sales	$1,000	$5,500	$4,500	$3,500	$14,500
5	Average price					$ 4.50
6	Most recent price					$ 1.00

Figure 10.7. Right and wrong price calculations.

This one you can do in your head: 6,950 times $1 doesn't equal $14,500. But, if you just use the most recent price for cell F3...

$$= E3$$

...then it looks like your math is wrong. This, by the way, is another example of how good-looking forecasts can have dumb errors embedded in them.

So it turns out, I assume you agree, that the correct average price for the period is really the formula you see in the formula edit bar, near the top of Figure 10.7:

$$= F4/F2,$$

which is what you'd get by dividing the $14,500 total sales for the 4-month period by the 6,950 total units sold during those 4 months.

So, going back to the complete sales forecast in Figure 10.1 (and 2.2), the formula for the price for the first year doesn't take the average of the twelve prices. Instead, it divides the total sales value for the year by the total number of units sold for the full year.

Average price is wrong because 6,950 times $4.50 = 31,275
Most recent price is wrong because 6,950 times 1 = 6,950

However, even this correct formula can look bad, unless you add another fine point, which comes next: an IF clause protecting against the divide-by-zero error. We need that in case we have a row with no units sold in one year. That's our next example.

The Divide-by-Zero and the IF Clause in Formulas

Going back to that formula in Figure 2.3, it also contains an IF clause to deal with the possibility of zero values. That's there because of what you see in Figure 10.8. It shows what happens with our formula in any of these price cells when we have a row without sales. We get a divide-by-zero error.

Now aside from computers and circuitry and all, there's really no error there, or there ought not to be. Cell F3 ought to just show a zero. Since no units were sold, sales are zero and the average price is zero. But computers can't deal with dividing something by zero, because of some deep circuitry logic issues; so it ends up as an error instead of a zero.

And it's an annoying error too, because it flows to the rest of your business calculations. That error will prevent the rest of the forecast from working right with charts, or printing, or other things. So you have to avoid it.

Figure 10.9 shows you how to avoid this problem with a small improvement in the formula to rule out the divide-by-zero error. That's

F3		*fx*	=F4/F2			
◇	A	B	C	D	E	F
1		Month1	Month2	Month3	Month4	Total
2	Units	0	0	0	0	0
3	Price	$10.00	$5.00	$2.00	$1.00	#DIV/0!
4	Sales	$0	$0	$0	$0	$0

Figure 10.8. The divide-by-zero problem.

=IF(F4<>0,F4/F2,0)						
◇	A	B	C	D	E	F
1		Month1	Month2	Month3	Month4	Total
2	Units	0	0	0	0	0
3	Price	$10.00	$5.00	$2.00	$1.00	$0.00
4	Sales	$0	$0	$0	$0	$0

Figure 10.9. IF clause corrects divide-by-zero problem.

exactly what I used in several price calculations, beginning with the prices in forecasts in chapter 2.

What this does with the simple IF clause is it catches the divide-by-zero error and isolates it. So as you look at the detail formula, you see a good example of the IF clause in a spreadsheet.

1. It starts with the "=IF(" which is spreadsheet language for opening up an IF function.
2. The way the IF function works is that the spreadsheet first checks the first phrase, which in this case is "F4<>0."
3. If that first phrase is correct, which would be true as long as the value in F4 is not zero, then it shows whatever is in the next phrase, which in this case is "F4/F2."
4. If that first phrase is not correct, which would be true when the value of cell F4 is zero, then it shows whatever is in the following phrase, which in this case is "0."

So what that works out to is three components: the first is the test, the second is what happens if the test is true, and the third what happens if the test is false. They are inside the IF() parentheses, set apart by commas.

More on Spreadsheet IF Logic

If you start to think about how that IF clause works in the previous section, you'll see that there can be a great deal of logic inside a simple sales forecast spreadsheet. The IF clause function is relatively simple to use, and it can be very powerful.

For example, you might use an IF formula to make average price or average cost a function of average volume, as in for example, just using hypothetically cell C36 in the simple sales forecast example in Figure 10.1 and 2.2:

$$= IF(C19>249,5,6.25),$$

which would make the unit cost only $5.00 per unit if the volume in row 19 is above 250, but $6.25 per unit if the volume in row 19 is less than 250.

Absolute References

The absolute reference is another common spreadsheet usage that you see first in chapter 2, and repeated throughout the book. One very common example is where a growth rate in column B is applied to a 12-month period in columns C through N. For example in Figure 10.10 (which is taken from the restaurant forecast in Figure 2.5) we have a growth rate in column B that's applied to the rest of the row.

In this one, the formula for cell D4 contains the absolute reference to column B4, specified by the use of the dollar sign:

$$= C4*(1+\$B4).$$

What the absolute reference means is that if we copy that cell's formula and paste it into another cell, the $B column reference doesn't change. So pasted into the next cell in the row, E4, the resulting formula would be

$$= D4*(1+\$B4),$$

which is the result of the absolute reference. Without those dollar signs, when D4 is copied and pasted into E4, the B4 growth rate reference would be to C4 instead of B4, which would be wrong.

You can use the dollar signs to lock in the row only or the column only, or both. In this first example, $B4 when copied into another cell would keep the reference to column B, but move the reference to row 4

=ROUND(C4*(1+$B4),0)				
◇	A	B	C	D	E
1	**Sales Forecast**				
2			Jan	Feb	Mar
3	**Unit Sales**				
4	Lunches	10%	200	220	242
5	Dinners	5%	450	473	497
6	Drinks	75%	488	520	554
7	Other		50	60	70
8	**Total Unit Sales**		1,188	1,273	1,363

Figure 10.10. Absolute references.

depending on which row the target cell is in. And a B$4 would lock the row 4, but allow moving the column B.

Rounding and the ROUND Function

The formula in Figure 10.10 also uses the ROUND function to manage the decimals. The "=ROUND(___,0)" portion of that formula tells it to take the results of the "C4*(1+$B4)" portion and round it to the nearest whole number. After all, that just makes sure you don't throw calculations off by having portions of a lunch, or portions of a unit.

I use rounding often. It comes up when you're multiplying or dividing numbers but you want to keep them to a certain level of decimals to make life easier. You'll note that I also sometimes round numbers to the nearest 100 or even 1,000. I like that in a forecast because it avoids the problem of false precision. Figure 10.11 shows how you can round down to decimals, or up to hundreds or thousands.

Rounding up is a good idea in a sales forecast. To show numbers in the nearest thousand, for example—as in cell B5 in the figure—makes it clearer that these are just educated guesses, not exact numbers.

Using Spreadsheet Graphics

In Figures 2.11 to 2.13 and then in chapter 6 again, I use spreadsheet graphics to show myself the relationship between numbers. This helps me a lot. How you do the line charts in the specific spreadsheet will vary, but all of the major spreadsheets will illustrate the numbers for you.

=ROUND($A$1,C4)

	A	B	C
1	6327.46754	6,327.00	0
2		6,327.50	1
3		6,327.47	2
4		6,300.00	-2
5		6,000.00	-3
6		10,000.00	-4

Figure 10.11. Rounding numbers.

Developing Your Date Lines

You may have noticed I almost always spread years or months across the top of the spreadsheet, in the first or second row. To optimize the spreadsheet's power, I usually use built-in spreadsheet date logic and formatting. It saves me typing.

For months, I start with the 15th day of the month. With most spreadsheets, that's just a matter of typing "1/15/2011" for January 15, 2011. Then I get the next month and create the flowing formula of referencing the previous and adding 30.4. For example, in this book, most of my spreadsheets start with 1/15/2011 in cell C2 and

$$= C2+30.4$$

in cell D2. Then I format both (using the spreadsheet number format facility) to show as "mmm" and copy the D cell to the right into the rest of the monthly header cells.

Learn to Copy Right

Select cells D through N for the second to the 12th month, then use the spreadsheet copy right or fill right feature to automatically copy. That saves time and saves typing.

Compound Average Growth Rate

The compound average growth rate, called CAGR, is another good formula to know. Especially for sales forecasts. I go into detail on CAGR in chapter 4, with the explanation surrounding Figure 4.2. Still, that example doesn't show the striking need for the correct growth calculations when you have variable growth, as in growth rates going up and down every year instead of staying steady, as in Figure 10.12.

In the second assumption set, one in which growth rates go up and down, the average growth as calculated by normal math averaging (you can see the formula in the edit bar, taking the average of cells C5 through G5) is way off. Because, surprising as it might seem, both of

=AVERAGE(C5:G5)

◇	A	B	C	D	E	F	G	H
1	Compound growth rate	2010	2011	2012	2013	2014	2015	CAGR
2	Assumption 1	$100.00	$110.00	$121.00	$133.10	$146.41	$161.05	10%
3	Annual Growth		10%	10%	10%	10%	10%	
4	Assumption 2	100	50	190	160	159	161.05	10%
5	Annual growth		-50%	280%	-16%	-1%	1%	43%

Figure 10.12. CAGR in changing growth situations.

these assumption lines have exactly the same compound average annual growth (CAGR): 10%.

The formula for cell H2, which you don't see in the figure, uses exactly the same CAGR formula shown in Figure 4.2: (last period/first period)^(1/number of periods)-1. In Cell H3 the formula is

$$= (G2/B2)^\wedge(1/5)-1.$$

And in Cell H4 the formula is

$$= (G4/B4)^\wedge(1/5)-1.$$

Sometimes that's not intuitive at all, but that's the magic of compounding, and the math is correct—in cells H2 and H4, that is, not at all in cell H5.

Use the Check Line When You Can

Figure 5.1 shows a check line built into a spreadsheet. I'm repeating that illustration here for your convenience, as Figure 10.13.

Cell F6 adds vertically, from F2 through F5. Cell F7 checks for spreadsheet errors by adding horizontally, cells B6 through E6. If they both have the same number, then you've checked the accuracy of the spreadsheet.

I've been shy about showing the check lines throughout this book, but I never work in a naked spreadsheet without them. Errors are hard to find, and they make you look particularly dumb when the client or boss spots them and you didn't.

There's no magic to figuring out how and where to put in some checks. Use your ingenuity.

	A	B	C	D	E	F
1		Q1-11	Q2-11	Q3-11	Q4-11	FY-2011
2	Cust A	$35	$45	$60	$40	$180
3	Cust B	$30	$30	$30	$30	$120
4	Cust C	$80	$100	$120	$110	$410
5	Others	$14	$18	$23	$19	$74
6	Total	$159	$193	$233	$199	$784
7	Check					784

Figure 10.13. Built-in check cell.

Differentiating Input vs. Calculated Cells

It might be harder to see in the black-and-white figures here, but when working with a real spreadsheet I always use shading or colors to make a visual reference to the difference between data cells and formula cells. In "real life" (meaning not constrained by colors available to me in a black-and-white printed book) I highlight input cells with dark blue or dark green colors. For purposes of illustration, in Figure 10.14 I've highlighted the input cells with a slight gray shading.

The idea is to make the structure of the forecast more obvious. Presumably you can see in that figure how the cells that are sitting there waiting for somebody to enter estimates as numbers, like input data, from the cells that calculate things.

Why does this matter? Because one of the very annoying weaknesses to standard spreadsheets is that they don't give you a visual clue to input vs. calculated cells. Unless, that is, you do that on purpose, as I'm suggesting here. And if you don't pay attention to which is which then you can end up messing up your formulas by typing over them.

	A	B	C	D	E	F	G
1		Month1	Month2	Month3	Month4	Total	CAGR
2	Units	100	1,100	2,250	3,500	6,950	227%
3	Price	$10.00	$5.00	$2.00	$1.00	$2.09	
4	Sales	$1,000	$5,500	$4,500	$3,500	$14,500	52%

Figure 10.14. Visual for input vs. calculated cells.

When I can, I use standard spreadsheet protection to clean this potential hotbed for errors up. In Microsoft Excel, each cell has a protected or not protected feature that you can access in the cell format areas. And if the worksheet is protected (you can do that without a password, just turn it on, make it easy to turn off), then the formula cells that are protected won't let you make that error.

Simplify by Dividing, But Be Careful

The forecast in chapter 4 shows several numbers with the annotation "(thousands)." The formula for cell C4 in Figure 4.6 is

$$= (\$B4*C2*C3)/1000000.$$

Adjusting the denominations as shown in that figure may be necessary at times, but it is always dangerous. It adds an important new source of potential error. Use adjustments like these only when needed, and with great care. When you adjust denominations like this, remember to specify denominations in row labels.

Simple Growth Rate

You had sales of 100 two years ago and 125 last year. What's the growth rate? Is it 25% because it's 25/100, or is it 20%? It's confusing.

This comes up in Figure 5.8. There is a standard for this, among forecasters. The percentage growth formulas are based on a simple standard formula:

$$\%Growth = (this\ year/last\ year) - 1.$$

In our puzzle question above, divide 125 by 120 and subtract 1. That's a 20% growth for that year, not 25%.

Lookup Function

I use a lookup function to deal with changing costs in chapter 7. In the strategic model, the unit cost of goods will go down as the units go up.

=VLOOKUP(D11,$A$21:$B$25,2)

◇	A	B	C	D
11	Our units	41	96	263
12	Revenue	$33,825	$74,400	$190,675
13	Fixed cost	$20,000	$21,000	$22,000
14	Unit cost	$500.00	$400.00	$250.00
15	Unit profit	$325	$375	$475
16	Gross profit	13,325	36,000	124,925
17	Net before taxes	(11,675)	(5,000)	2,925

20	Unit Cost Index	
21	0	500
22	50	400
23	100	300
24	250	250
25	500	200

Figure 10.15. The lookup table.

To mimic that behavior, I put a vertical look-up table into the model. That's in Figures 7.1 and 7.2; portions of them are combined here as Figure 10.15.

So you can see how the lookup function works in cell D14, which is highlighted in the figure. The formula is

= *VLOOKUP(D11,$A$21:$B25,2),*

so it looks up the value in D11, which is 263. Then it finds the vertical column of the lookup range A21:B25, and picks up the value where 263 fits. It's between 250 and 500, so it calculates that as $250, which is in the second column of that lookup range. So the unit cost is $250.

Index

Note: The italicized *f* following page numbers refers to figures.